KFK KINGFISHER KNOWLEDGE

ARCHAEOLOGY

KFK KINGFISHER KNOWLEDGE

ARCHAEOLOGY

Trevor Barnes

Foreword by
Tony Robinson

KINGFISHER

Editor: Catherine Brereton
Senior designer: Peter Clayman
Cover designer: Anthony Cutting
Picture research manager: Cee Weston-Baker
Consultant: Dr Miles Russell, Bournemouth University
Senior production controller: Debbie Otter
DTP co-ordinator: Sarah Pfitzner
Artwork archivists: Wendy Allison, Jenny Lord
Proofreader: Sheila Clewley
Indexer: Sue Lightfoot

KINGFISHER

Kingfisher Publications Plc, New Penderel House,
283–288 High Holborn, London WC1V 7HZ
www.kingfisherpub.com

First published by Kingfisher Publications Plc 2004
First published in this format in 2006

10 9 8 7 6 5 4 3 2 1

1TR/0706/TWP/MA(MA)/130ENSOMA/F

ISBN-13: 978 0 7534 1056 1
ISBN-10: 0 7534 1056 7

NOTE TO READERS

The website addresses listed in this book are correct at the time of going to print.
However, due to the ever-changing nature of the internet, website addresses and
content can change. Websites can contain links that are unsuitable for children.
The publisher cannot be held responsible for changes in website addresses or
content, or for information obtained through third-party websites. We strongly
advise that internet searches should be supervised by an adult.

GO FURTHER...
INFORMATION PANEL KEY:

 websites and
further reading

 career paths

 places to visit

Contents

Foreword

The trouble with archaeology is that it's so difficult to spell. A lot of people think that a word that's got 'aeo' in the middle of it must refer to something so complicated that only huge-brained people could possibly understand it. But anyone who thinks this is completely wrong. Archaeology is basically pretty simple. It's the way we can hurtle back into history to discover how people lived hundreds, even thousands of years ago. And how do we do that? By using detective work. Archaeologists are like the police at a crime scene. They slowly and carefully piece together all the little bits of evidence they find on a site in order to work out what was going on there in the dim and distant past.

It may sound quite a glamorous job, but this evidence is seldom valuable or beautiful to look at. It's rubbish. It's the old junk people have lost, thrown away or buried throughout history. Don't be fooled by Lara Croft or Indiana Jones. Archaeologists aren't treasure hunters who smash up ancient temples or blow up pyramids in order to snatch some jewel-encrusted casket. Most archaeology is about sifting through broken bits of old pots, handfuls of charred seeds or pieces of crumbling wood in order to work out what the lives of ordinary people were like in days gone by.

Even the tiniest speck of dust can be important. Eighty years ago, when the English archaeologist Howard Carter discovered the tomb of the Egyptian pharaoh Tutankhamun, he swept it clean before inviting the press in to photograph his fabulous finds. Nowadays archaeologists would give their eye teeth to get their hands on that dust. All those tiny dead insects, the strands of hair and the little fragments of material that ended up in the dustpan would tell us far more about ancient Egypt than a hundred gold chariots.

In Carter's time, archaeology was all about digging. But today three weeks on an archaeological site generates three months of activity in the laboratory. There are specialists who can date a piece of wood from the shape of the tree-rings, others who can tell whether a site was once wooded, boggy or covered in trees from examining the shells of long-dead snails. There are people who can work out exactly where a piece of pottery originally came from by looking at the tiny flecks of stone in it, and others who can find out the sex and age of a skeleton and what diseases its owner suffered from.

Digging is still a major part of archaeology. In the 21st century, however, we're much more careful about where we dig. Archaeology is part of our environment. I don't expect you'd dream of chopping down a valued tree or stealing birds' eggs, because you know you'd be damaging something precious. But some people still damage burial sites or dig coins out of archaeological sites and pocket them. Most of them don't realize that they're destroying something irreplaceable. Archaeologists do. They only dig part of a site, and leave the rest for future generations. They record what they find and where they found it, and make sure everything is properly labelled and sent to a museum.

Archaeologists are time travellers, detectives and friends of the environment. Sounds good, doesn't it? Get stuck into this book and join them in exploring some of the most amazing archaeological sites in the world.

Tony Robin

Tony Robinson – president, Young Archaeologists' Club and presenter of Channel 4's *Time Team*

CHAPTER 1

Machu Picchu, an ancient Inca city high in the
Andes mountains, rediscovered in CE1911

What is archaeology?

Archaeology is partly about things but mainly about people. The excitement of archaeology lies in building up a picture of human life hundreds, even thousands of years ago, by making connections between things found in the ground and the people who left them there long ago. Often the physical objects left behind are simple things – tools, toys, weapons, household goods and coins. They may be fragments of buildings – a piece of wall, barn or road – or great structures such as Egyptian temples, Greek amphitheatres, or even whole cities like the ancient Inca capital of Machu Picchu. But what they all have in common is that they have survived, while the people who made them are long since dead. If these remains could speak, what exciting tales they would tell. Archaeology tries to be their voice.

Introducing archaeology

Archaeology is the hands-on study of the past. It involves the excavation or examination of sites and the careful study and analysis of material remains left by people who once lived or worked there. Many of the finds unearthed go on public display, but archaeology is not just about collecting objects. For archaeologists it is about understanding. Finding a treasure in a 5,000-year-old pyramid is exciting. More exciting still is understanding why people put such a treasure there in the first place.

▲ General Augustus Pitt-Rivers (1827–1900) excavated prehistoric sites in southern England. He helped pave the way for modern techniques.

When did it begin?

People have always been interested in the past, and revered objects and places that were important to their ancestors. We know that King Nebuchadnezzar of Babylon (see pages 32–33) excavated parts of his city over 2,500 years ago. Babylonian princesses kept the antique objects in their own private rooms. In the 16th and 17th centuries CE, there was a fashion for 'cabinets of curiosities' in which rich people could display interesting or valuable objects. But archaeology as the systematic process of understanding the past did not begin until the late 18th century CE.

The start of modern archaeology

In CE1784, the man who was to become the third President of the United States, Thomas Jefferson (1743–1826), pioneered a new approach to excavation. While examining native American burial mounds on his land, he decided that simply digging deeper and deeper to see what objects came to light was imprecise. So he cut a large slice out of one mound and analyzed the various levels, or strata, of material. He carried out a scientific examination of the soil and the skeletons. Scientific thought became as important as spadework.

▲ The American statesman and thinker, Thomas Jefferson, is often referred to as the father of modern archaeology. He was one of the first to take a systematic, scientific approach to excavation.

▼ This imaginary scene shows archaeologists excavating the ruins of an ancient classical temple. Like the fictional archaeologist and adventurer Indiana Jones, they are unearthing splendid treasures. But archaeology is just as much about examining rubbish and debris, and the humdrum sites are just as important as the spectacular in building a picture of life in the past.

Archaeology and adventure

In the 19th and early 20th centuries, major excavations were taking place in the Middle East, and archaeology could seem like adventure. Men such as Heinrich Schliemann (see page 16) used their personal wealth to finance expeditions. On the other side of the world, the American diplomat John Lloyd Stephens (1805–1852) led explorations deep into the Mexican jungle, where he discovered the ruined cities of the ancient Mayan people who had lived there centuries earlier.

◄ Archaeology takes objects such as this amulet discovered in the grave of a 6th-century BCE Celtic chief in Hochdorf, Germany, and asks where they fit into a picture of the past. Burying such a beautiful, well-crafted object suggests that this society placed great importance on funerary rituals.

A scientific discipline

Archaeology is certainly exciting, but it is not really about adventure and treasure. It is a scientific discipline which uses the objects unearthed at dig sites – including everyday items and rubbish as well as magnificent treasures – as the basis for study. Once archaeologists have collected the objects, they get to work in laboratories and studies, examining the remains and making sense of all the evidence. Even Indiana Jones (based on the real-life American archaeologist Hiram Bingam, 1875–1956) is portrayed as a scholar, teacher and university professor.

What do archaeologists do?

Many people study the past. Archaeologists like to get their hands on it! Of course they read written accounts of earlier civilizations, but they rely chiefly on the physical objects left behind by people in the past. Archaeologists explore a site, sifting through evidence and making a detailed examination of clues. Even the tiniest pieces of evidence can help them build up a picture of life long ago.

◀ Some of the things that archaeologists study are spectacular. Here they are measuring moai, the vast stone statues on Easter Island in the Pacific Ocean. These remarkable statues were built between 1600 and 100BCE.

Examining a site

Once archaeologists have identified an area they believe contains evidence of the past, they start a detailed examination, or dig. Usually, they dig a narrow section called a trench. Larger sites are divided up so that a team can carry out a systematic examination. Archaeologists note carefully where objects have been discovered and mark them on plans and drawings. They take great care not to damage fragile objects or lose track of exactly where things are found – an object's position is just as important as the object itself. They use simple tools, such as trowels and brushes, to remove soil or sand. Sometimes, more sophisticated machinery is called for, such as radar or echo-sounding equipment. By sending electrical charges into the ground, these detect objects hidden beneath the earth.

Layers of time

One of the main questions archaeologists need to answer is how old is the evidence they are digging up? The dig site itself can help. On sites where there has been constant human activity, the ground level rises over the years as people build on top of what previous generations have left behind. Material builds up in layers called strata. Each layer dates from a different period in history, and studying them helps archaeologists to work out the relative ages of the objects they find. Other techniques are also useful. Carbon dating measures radioactivity to tell the age of organic objects such as bone and plant material. Scientists can also tell the age of a wooden object from tree ring patterns.

▲ These decayed timbers may not look very exciting at first glance, but an archaeologist examining them can learn a wealth of information. They belong to a merchant ship dating back to ᴄᴇ1465. It sank when it had just returned from Portugal with a cargo of cork bark and is the only surviving vessel of its kind. It was discovered during excavation works for a new riverside building in Newport, Wales, in 2002.

▶ This diagram shows layers of material, or strata, in an imaginary trench in Britain. In the top layer are modern items of rubbish such as a bottle, can and plastic bag. Further down are crockery and clay pipes from the 18th century, cannon balls and a sword from the 17th century and a medieval pot. Then there are a comb and spearhead from Viking times (late ᴄᴇ700s) and a gold buckle and other jewellery from the Anglo-Saxon period (c. ᴄᴇ440–1066). At the base the archaeologist has found a Roman helmet and beaker (c. ᴄᴇ100). No real trench would be so clearly layered or contain so many treasures, though!

History and prehistory

Archaeologists study such a vast timespan – from over 10,000 years ago until the present day – that they need to divide it into periods. 'History' is the time for which we have written records as well as physical remains – since about 3000ʙᴄᴇ in Mesopotamia but later elsewhere in the world. 'Prehistory' is the time before this and is divided up into the Stone Age, Bronze Age and Iron Age, named after the main materials used in these periods. Before 8000ʙᴄᴇ, people made tools out of stone. Around 4000ʙᴄᴇ, they began to develop bronze items, and later still (c. 1400ʙᴄᴇ) they started to use iron. It is impossible to date these periods accurately as they vary throughout the world, and even overlap.

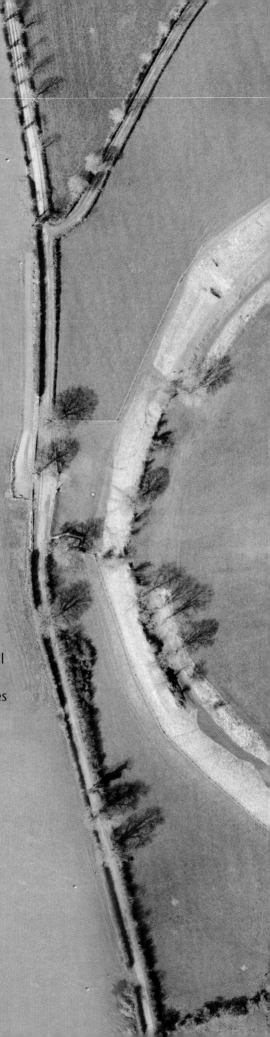

Where is archaeology?

Evidence of the past is everywhere. Sometimes it is right under our noses – a Saxon church at the end of an English lane, the ruins of a Crusader castle on a Middle Eastern hilltop, or a pueblo town in the American southwest. But sometimes the evidence is hidden from view and archaeologists need to search for less obvious clues.

▲ This remarkably well-preserved corpse of an Iron Age man, over 2,000 years old, was found by chance in a peat bog in Jutland, Denmark, in 1950. A noose around his neck indicates that he died by hanging. His stomach still contained his last meal – wild grains and grasses.

Physical remains

Ancient ruins provide us with the most visible clues to the past. The physical remains of buildings, whether in brick, stone or timber, tell us that people once lived or worked there. The archaeologist's task is to explore more thoroughly. Slowly excavating the site, teams will carefully search for artefacts before listing and storing them for later analysis.

Clues from the land

Sometimes what remains of an earlier construction is not immediately obvious. Perhaps stones have been removed to make other buildings elsewhere or timbers have rotted away. Even if nothing is visible at ground level, a view from a different angle can tell a different story. Odd marks on the earth – hedges growing in perfect circles or in dead straight lines following the contours of man-made ditches, for example – show that human hands have been at work. Archaeologists use technology such as aerial photography, echo-sounding equipment, geophysical surveys and satellite photography to find out more about what is buried beneath the surface.

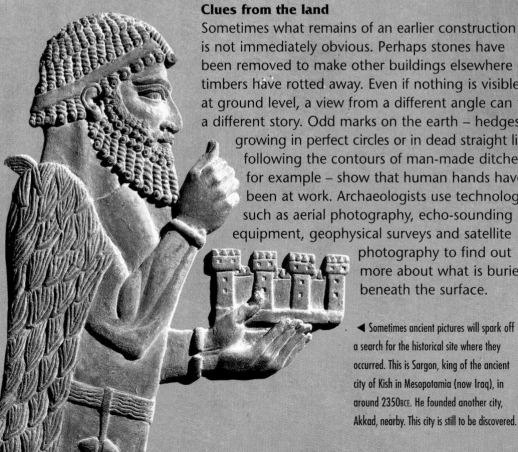

◄ Sometimes ancient pictures will spark off a search for the historical site where they occurred. This is Sargon, king of the ancient city of Kish in Mesopotamia (now Iraq), in around 2350BCE. He founded another city, Akkad, nearby. This city is still to be discovered.

▼ Detail that could easily be missed at ground level becomes clear when viewed from the air. An aerial view of Navan fort in Northern Ireland shows that this fortress (dating from 700BCE) has a protective ditch and is ringed by a defensive bank.

Written evidence

Records such as maps and historical documents also tell us that particular sites have been associated with human activity over the years. A map produced in the 18th century, for example, may show a building which is no longer standing. But excavation may reveal that its foundations still remain beneath the surface of the soil – and tell us whether it has been used for different purposes over the centuries.

Chance finds

The most exciting discoveries are often made by chance. In 1940, boys walking in woods at Lascaux in southwest France found prehistoric cave paintings that had been hidden for 15,000 years (see pages 20–21). Sometimes, freak weather conditions give chance a helping hand. In 1991, a partial thaw of a glacier in northern Italy revealed the body of a Bronze Age man, perfectly preserved by the ice for over 5,000 years.

▲ This map of Tenochtitlan (see pages 50–51) exaggerates the size of the sacred enclosure at the heart of the city, which was marvelled at by the Spanish who made the map in the 16th century. Maps such as this are full of clues for archaeologists.

Bits and pieces

No object is too big or too small for an archaeologist to study. Whether it is a whole city that has lain undisturbed in the mountains for centuries or a coin no bigger than a thumbnail, each object that comes to light is a vital clue to the past. An archaeologist is a kind of historical detective, piecing together clues to try to build a complete picture. But every time a new piece of evidence emerges, the picture changes. Questions may be answered or new mysteries emerge. Far from staying still, our understanding of the past is constantly evolving.

Three-dimensional jigsaws

Archaeologists love jigsaws – in three dimensions and with no pictures to guide them. They may find a small piece of pottery as they excavate a site. Then they find another, and another, and before long they are piecing together fragments of a jar that was used 2,000 years ago. Careful analysis of the inside of the pot will show what it was used for – storing grain, water, wine or olive oil perhaps. Some pottery fragments are very elaborate. Vases from Athens in the 6th century BCE, for example, show scenes from everyday Athenian life and tell us much about society in ancient Greece.

▲ An archaeologist examines everyday rubbish from long ago – an oyster shell mound unearthed along the banks of the river at the site of St Mary's City, believed to be the earliest settlement in modern-day Maryland, USA. Shellfish such as oysters were an important food source in early riverside settlements.

▲ This silver coin was minted during the time of Ptolemy I, who reigned over Egypt from 304BCE. Coins are easy to date because the ruler shown will have been historically documented. They may be found thousands of miles from their origin, shedding light on patterns of trade.

► Pictures from the past show us how people worked or played and what they looked like. Sometimes, a single vivid picture can speak louder than words, giving us a real sense of connection with an ancient civilization. This wall painting from the palace of Knossos (see pages 34–35) shows two boys boxing.

► It's not just the important buildings and precious objects that survive for centuries. Unusual circumstances, such as burial by volcanic ash, can mean remarkable finds – like this bowl of olives found at Pompeii (see pages 42–43), preserved for nearly 2,000 years.

Human remains

Sometimes the fragments archaeologists study are human remains. Skulls, bones and teeth can tell us a lot about the injuries people suffered, the kinds of food they ate and how they died. Burial mounds, graves and tombs are rich in this kind of detail. The way in which the dead were buried can help us build up a picture of how the living organized their societies. Graves often contain artefacts such as jewellery and weapons, and give us an indication of what the people buried there thought about death. Many believed that death was the start of a new life somewhere else – so they buried the dead with objects they thought would help on the journey through the afterlife.

Rubbish

While treasures and riches are exciting and important, much of what archaeologists find is rubbish – objects lost, broken or thrown away as part of everyday life. This rubbish often tells us the most about a site and the people who lived there. What might future generations make of the bits and pieces you throw away?

▼ Ornamental objects can tell us about a society's beliefs and customs. This head depicting a coyote warrior, an important figure, is from the Toltec civilization, from South America over 3,000 years ago.

Famous finds

▲ This mask, discovered at Mycenae, Greece, was believed by Heinrich Schliemann (1822–1890) to belong to the legendary king Agamemnon (born c. 1140BCE). It surprised the world as it suggested that a figure from legend might have a basis in historical fact.

All over the world, archaeologists are discovering interesting objects that tell them more and more about the past. Usually their discoveries are so specialized that only a handful of scholars and professionals ever get to hear of them. But from time to time, major discoveries are made which are so unusual, rich or unexpected that they make headline news across the world.

The Sutton Hoo ship burial

In 1939, at Sutton Hoo in Suffolk, England, archaeologists excavating Anglo-Saxon burial mounds made a remarkable discovery. They unearthed the remains of a 7th-century CE ship, which contained a rich collection of treasures, and may once have carried the body of King Raedwald (died CE625). Long ago, when the king died, a ship was hauled out of the water onto dry land. The king's body was placed inside a chamber in the ship, which was loaded with precious objects before being buried. When it was discovered, the timber frame had rotted away, but the treasures remained.

▶ No definite evidence of a body was discovered at Sutton Hoo, but this magnificent helmet helps us imagine the king. It would once have protected him in battle.

The treasures

The objects inside the ship at Sutton Hoo were in a poor state of preservation, but the treasures give us a rare glimpse into the splendours of the Saxon royal court. Gold jewellery inlaid with coloured glass, belt buckles, clasps, shields, helmets, weapons, coins and drinking horns (all pictured below) hint at the importance and the status of the king.

Similar precious objects were unearthed in 1978 in the grave of a 6th-century BCE Celtic chieftan in Hochdorf, Germany. These included drinking horns, weapons, jewellery and a decorated bronze couch. Elaborate burials such as these, of individuals of high status, help archaeologists understand how earlier societies organized themselves, and honoured a powerful king or chief who ruled over them.

▶ The Rosetta Stone is a polished stone engraved with three versions of the same text, discovered in Egypt in 1799. Later, in 1822, the archaeologist François Champollion (1790–1832) used his knowledge of ancient Egyptian and ancient Greek to decipher the hieroglyphs on the stone. Thousands of other Egyptian hieroglyphs have been decoded since then.

A hidden city

Other headline-grabbing finds include the discovery, in 1911, of a whole city that had been hidden for 500 years. Machu Picchu, named after the mountain that rises above it, was a fortified city high in the Andes of South America (see picture on page 7). It was built by the Incas, but was never found by the Spanish, who invaded in the 16th century CE. Its palace, its temple to the sun and its lofty location ensured that it became a modern-day wonder of the world.

Nothing too small

Sometimes one small object can have enormous implications for our understanding of the past. The Rosetta Stone, for example, revolutionized the way the world understood early Egyptian civilization. It is a stone engraved with three versions of the same text. One was written in ancient Egyptian, one in ancient Greek and the third in Egyptian picture writing known as hieroglyphs, which no modern person had been able to read. It proved to be a key to this previously mysterious writing system.

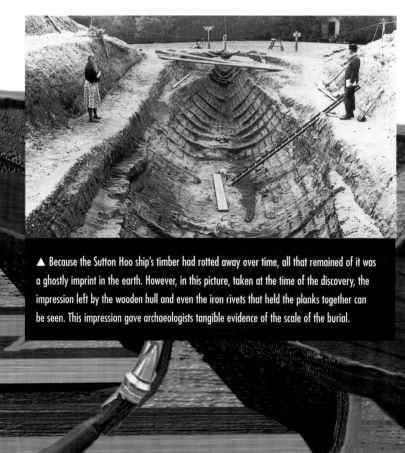

▲ Because the Sutton Hoo ship's timber had rotted away over time, all that remained of it was a ghostly imprint in the earth. However, in this picture, taken at the time of the discovery, the impression left by the wooden hull and even the iron rivets that held the planks together can be seen. This impression gave archaeologists tangible evidence of the scale of the burial.

▲ In the 8th century CE, the Moors of north Africa invaded what is now Spain. They were a cultured people, who valued fine architecture, and many of their buildings survive to this day. The Alhambra palace was the last fortress of the Moorish kings of Granada.

▼ In an impressive salvage operation to save the priceless ruins of Pharaoh Rameses II's temples at Abu Simbel from flooding, the statues and columns were sliced into sections and physically removed to higher ground. They were then reassembled out of the way of the rising water behind the Aswan Dam.

Changing times

Our lives do not stand still for a moment. They are constantly moving and changing in a series of events. Over thousands of years, change is enormous. Cultures grow and decline, countries go to war and conquer one another, and people develop new technologies and ways of living. The things people leave behind, by contrast, are motionless and lifeless. In bringing the past back to life it is as if archaeologists are creating a moving picture from a series of snapshots.

Change and conquest

Change is rarely sudden, as civilizations rise and fall and societies build on what went before. Change has often been accompanied by violence, as one culture conquers another. For example, the Norman Conquest of England in CE1066 brought huge changes to Anglo-Saxon life, adding new words, architecture and systems of government to what had gone before. Elsewhere in Europe, for seven centuries the Moors of north Africa left their mark on Spain, until they were driven out of their last stronghold of Granada in CE1492.

Difficult choices

Governments often have to choose between saving an archaeological site or developing over it. In 1959, the Egyptian government had to decide whether the building of a dam at Aswan was more important than the preservation of the temples at Abu Simbel, which would have been submerged as the Nile valley flooded. As a compromise, the temples themselves were moved. A similar project is underway to save the Ba Wang temple in China, when a dam due to be completed in 2009 will flood the Yangtze.

War

Throughout history, cities have been destroyed by conflict, and the evidence of past battles is all around us. War is not confined to the past, and still brings destruction to sites of great archaeological importance. Fighting in the former Yugoslavia in the early 1990s destroyed many ancient and well-loved religious buildings. Perhaps the most dramatic act of destruction there took place in Mostar (now in Bosnia) in 1993, when the beautiful 16th-century bridge spanning the river collapsed after months of shelling.

▲ Civil disorder in Iraq during the war of 2003 resulted in the looting of Baghdad's museum and the destruction or plunder of many of its exhibits, some of the most ancient and precious artefacts in the world.

Sometimes it is claimed that important cultural sites have been deliberately targeted by attackers, since this can have a profound impact on a city's people.

Everyday change

Buildings do not last for ever, and in time our own houses will crumble and fall. Should their history be erased to make way for a road or an airport runway? And what should happen when companies building a skyscraper in a European city discover the ruins of a Roman temple or a medieval theatre in the foundations? In many countries agreements have been reached that allow archaeologists to examine a site before any new construction work gets underway.

▶ Political change can influence the fate of major archaeological sites. In 1975, conservation work was underway on the magnificent and world-famous statues of the Buddha at Bamiyan in Afghanistan. In 2001, despite worldwide criticism, the extreme Islamic group, the Taliban, destroyed the statues (below).

Where next?

Archaeologists are discovering more about the past all the time. Every day new objects are discovered and new sites excavated. But archaeology is not simply about collecting more things. It is about extending the boundaries of what we know about the past. It involves everything from improving methods of measuring to developing new theories; from exploring new methods of finding, examining and storing evidence to displaying it in exciting ways.

▲ The prehistoric cave paintings at Lascaux in southwest France attracted so many visitors in the decades after their discovery in CE1940 that the images were under threat from changes in temperature, humidity and even the chemicals in people's breath! To preserve them, the cave was closed to the public in 1963 and a full-scale replica, known as Lascaux II, was built nearby as a visitor attraction.

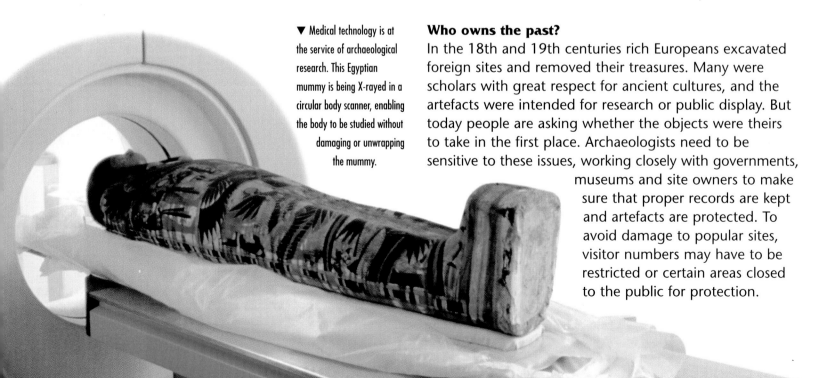

▼ Medical technology is at the service of archaeological research. This Egyptian mummy is being X-rayed in a circular body scanner, enabling the body to be studied without damaging or unwrapping the mummy.

Who owns the past?
In the 18th and 19th centuries rich Europeans excavated foreign sites and removed their treasures. Many were scholars with great respect for ancient cultures, and the artefacts were intended for research or public display. But today people are asking whether the objects were theirs to take in the first place. Archaeologists need to be sensitive to these issues, working closely with governments, museums and site owners to make sure that proper records are kept and artefacts are protected. To avoid damage to popular sites, visitor numbers may have to be restricted or certain areas closed to the public for protection.

▶ We all have evidence of our ancestors in our DNA. These people in Colombia are likely to be descended from Spanish invaders as well as native American people.

Presentation

Archaeology is not just for archaeologists. It is for all of us. So archaeologists are exploring new ways of presenting their findings to the public. They can use the latest computer graphics to rebuild ancient landscapes in breathtaking detail, or recreate past worlds on television or film. Sometimes a historic building is actually rebuilt or restored. For a more hands-on experience, museums such as the Jorvik Viking Centre in York, England, have a sort of archaeological theme park, giving visitors the chance to experience the sights, sounds and even smells of a place in centuries past.

▲ It's not just the very distant past that interests archaeologists – and the public. Here, visitors to the National Railway Museum in York, England, prepare to take a ride on a working reconstruction of the *Rocket*, one of the earliest steam trains, which made its first journey in 1829.

New technology

Developments in science and technology mean that archaeologists have ever sharper tools at their disposal for examining evidence of the past. Improvements in the quality of satellite imaging, ground-penetrating radar and scientific dating methods will help reveal more about archaeological sites. The latest chemical and biological techniques allow scientists to uncover minute details of everyday life – pollen grains in household waste or in the long-decayed contents of a person preserved in a peat bog, for example, can tell us a lot about their diet and environment. Scientists can even study the traces of fat in an ancient pot and work out which foods were cooked in it.

Archaeologists can use DNA testing to find out if groups of bodies found together are related. They can even study today's people to clear up past mysteries. In Colombia, DNA research has shown that today's population is largely descended from European men and native American women. This suggests that when the Spanish conquered the region they killed the local males and married the local women. This supports contemporary evidence of a massacre.

Our recent past

Archaeologists today are excavating remains of the much more recent past. The 19th century produced great inventions and machinery which are now outdated. Farm and factory tools made just 100 or 200 years ago may be mysterious to us now. Industrial archaeologists can learn much from these objects. They study how changes in transport and technology affected people's daily lives.

SUMMARY OF CHAPTER 1: WHAT IS ARCHAEOLOGY?

Digging for the past

Archaeology is the study of the physical remains of the past. As we have seen, it involves many different skills. Working on a dig and excavating a site, for example, can be physically hard, time-consuming work. Both the site and the artefacts then have to be analyzed carefully and scientifically. Archaeology also requires intellectual skill and imagination. Archaeologists take as their starting point the material remains of individuals, communities, cultures and whole civilizations and then go on to ask important questions about the past. How did people – whose faces we have never seen except perhaps in frescoes or mosaics, and whose names we shall never know – live their lives? And how have those lives shaped our own?

The Battersea shield, an elaborate Iron Age artefact found in London, England, dating from 350–50BCE

Displaying and explaining

Rather than collecting (or even plundering!) artefacts for their own personal satisfaction, archaeologists are responsible for sharing their discoveries with the world. They carefully preserve sites and objects for future generations and display their findings in imaginative ways. Where to display them can sometimes be controversial. Should artefacts be removed and displayed out of their original context in museums? In the case of Aboriginal artefacts from Australia, Aborigine people have said no and asked for the return of their cultural heritage. Many other artefacts are the subject of debates about ownership and about how precious objects should be preserved.

All the time, archaeologists are turning their attention to new places and discovering more about familiar places. Their purpose is to unearth the objects with sensitivity and, in the process, to add bit by bit to our store of knowledge. Perhaps the greatest excitement of all is knowing that there are more treasures waiting to be found, more mysteries waiting to be explained and more stories to be told.

Go further...

 Dig out more information about archaeology:
www.digonsite.com

Find out the latest archaeological stories and discoveries:
www.bbc.co.uk/history/archaeology

Join the Young Archaeologists' Club:
www.britarch.ac.uk/yac/index.html

Learn about digs in your local area:
www.channel4.com/history/timeteam/index.html

Awesome Archaeology by Nick Arnold (Scholastic, 2001)

Archaeology: Discovering the Past by John Orna-Ornstein (British Museum Press, 2002)

 Archaeologist
Studies the past by working on dig sites and examining the physical remains of past settlements.

Forensic scientist
Uses the latest scientific techniques to examine ancient human remains.

Historian
Reads and writes about people, places and events from the past.

Tour guide
Accompanies visitors around archaeological sites.

Volunteer
Helps local archaeologists with their excavation and conservation work.

 Visit the British Museum to see artefacts including the Sutton Hoo hoard and the Rosetta Stone:
Great Russell Street,
London WC1B 3DG, UK.
Telephone: +44 (0) 20 7323 8482
www.thebritishmuseum.ac.uk/index.html

Take a trip back in time to a Viking town at the Jorvik Viking Centre, York:
Coppergate, York YO1 9WT, UK.
Telephone: +44 (0) 1904 643 211
www.jorvik-viking-centre.co.uk

See the replica cave paintings at Lascaux II, Montignac, France:
www.culture.gouv.fr:80/culture/arcnat/lascaux/en/

Detail from the 'Standard of Ur' (peace side), c. 2600BCE

CHAPTER 2

Touching the past

There are hundreds of thousands of archaeological sites in the world. All of them add to our understanding of the past. But some stand out from the rest. They may be very old, like the remains of Catal Hüyük in Turkey, for example, which gave us a clearer picture of life in prehistoric times; or extremely rich in detail, like the ruins of Pompeii; or they may be places, like some battlefield sites,

where archaeology challenges existing views of history. Some sites are simply spectacular, such as the tomb of Tutankhamun in Egypt, which amazed the world with its treasures. You can look in detail at a selection of outstanding sites in this chapter. One day you, too, may visit some of the sites and, like archaeologists before you, experience the thrill of touching fragments of the past with your own hands.

◄ Tools and weapons like this flint arrowhead of the palaeolithic period developed over millions of years. Dating them accurately is extremely difficult since the palaeolithic or early Stone Age stretches from 2 million years ago to about 13,000 years ago. The refinement and precision of this one, from Slovakia in Europe, suggests a date towards the end of this period.

● Little Bighorn

● Cahokia

Tenochtitlan ●

Sites around the world

All over the world there are places where people have lived, worked, built homes and cities, fought battles, practised religion and art and buried their dead. There are hundreds of thousands of archaeological sites, rich in evidence of the past. This map shows the places that you can explore in the rest of this chapter.

Before settlements

For the earliest people, life was a constant struggle for survival. There were no luxuries – only the necessities of food, water, clothing and shelter. For thousands of years people were nomadic, moving from place to place in order to hunt for animals and to gather berries and nuts. We know them as hunter-gatherers. Some made their homes in caves. The artefacts that have survived from these times include tools and weapons (such as axeheads and arrowheads), carved ornaments, jewellery and very few remains of buildings.

The first settlements

The first farmers settled nearly 10,000 years ago in the Middle East. Communities chose where to live, and built permanent houses. Similar developments happened slightly later elsewhere. Gradually, all over the world, sophisticated civilizations arose – first in Egypt, Mesopotamia and China. Later, settlements grew in Europe, Peru and east Africa. As civilizations have risen and fallen, they have left behind the wealth of fascinating material evidence that archaeologists study today.

◄ Before people made permanent settlements they lived a nomadic lifestyle, wandering from place to place. Little remains of the temporary homes they built, but early rock art depicting things of importance, like this 10,000-year-old collection of hunting drawings from Namibia, Africa, has survived. Similar cave paintings exist on every continent.

► Ceremonial buildings like the royal mausoleum carved out of the cliffs of the desert are all that remain of the city of Petra, Jordan, which was at the height of its power between 50BCE and CE70, and provide archaeologists with a wealth of information. Many cultures flourished in the Middle East at this time and Petra was at the centre of important trading routes.

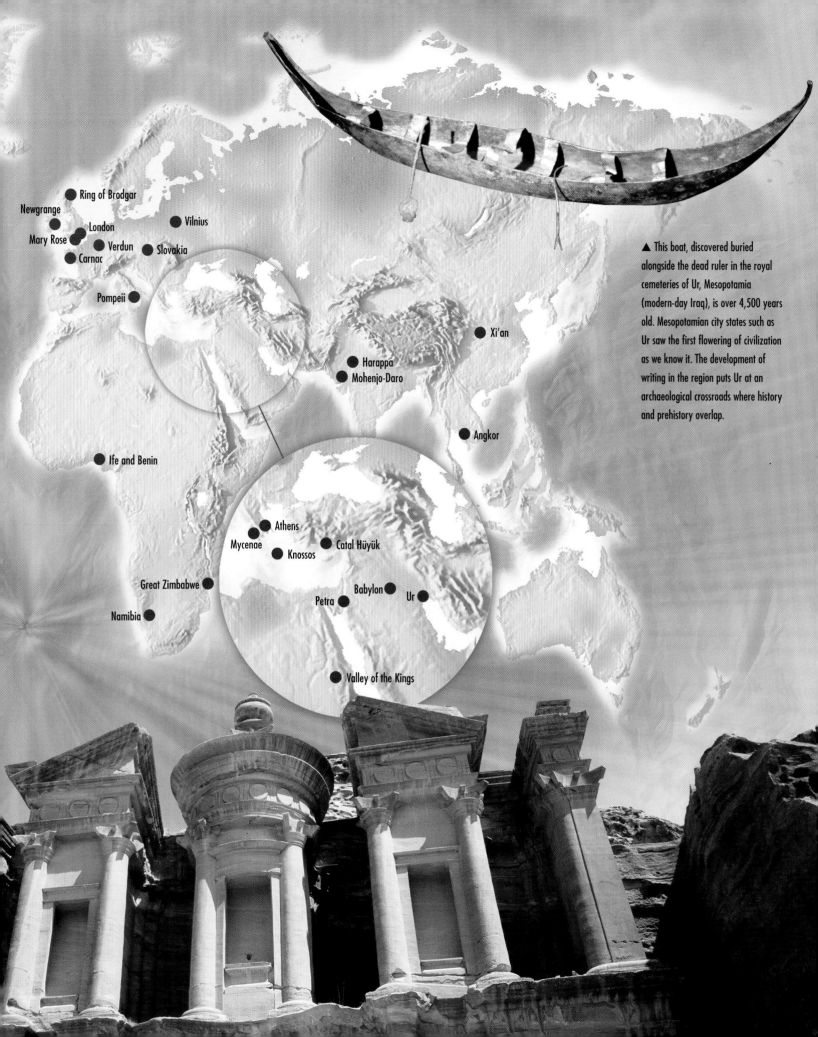

Ring of Brodgar

Newgrange

London

Mary Rose

Verdun

Carnac

Vilnius

Slovakia

Pompeii

Xi'an

Harappa

Mohenjo-Daro

Angkor

Ife and Benin

Athens

Mycenae

Knossos

Catal Hüyük

Great Zimbabwe

Petra Babylon Ur

Namibia

Valley of the Kings

▲ This boat, discovered buried alongside the dead ruler in the royal cemeteries of Ur, Mesopotamia (modern-day Iraq), is over 4,500 years old. Mesopotamian city states such as Ur saw the first flowering of civilization as we know it. The development of writing in the region puts Ur at an archaeological crossroads where history and prehistory overlap.

Catal Hüyük

▲ This terracotta figurine of a large woman is believed to be a fertility symbol, representing a 'mother goddess' who was worshipped for the rich harvests she could bring to the people.

For thousands of years, as we have seen, people lived a nomadic lifestyle. Then, around 9,000 years ago, the hunter-gatherers began to choose where they wanted to live and to build structures in which the whole community could lead more settled lives. Catal Hüyük in modern day Turkey is one of the earliest of these towns, and it gives us a fascinating glimpse into the lives of men and women who first began to domesticate their surroundings so long ago.

The discovery

In 1961, the British archaeologist James Mellaart (born 1925) travelled to southern Turkey to excavate an artificial earth mound (*hüyük* in Turkish) which he had discovered three years earlier, while surveying the Konya Plain of Anatolia. As he and his team removed layer after layer of soil, they found the remains of a Stone Age town, which had been home to between 5,000 and 6,000 people at around 6000BCE. The site covered an area about the same size as 50 football pitches and would, at its height, have been one of the most densely populated places on earth.

◄ The bull, featured in many wall paintings, is a male image of fertility. Fertility was vital to a community which relied on agriculture and hunting for its survival and prosperity. Hunting was important for the food and skins it provided and for the shared ritual it offered the people of the town.

A farming community

Mellaart's excavations (and later ones) unearthed evidence of a highly advanced farming community. The region was fertile at this time and the people of Catal Hüyük took full advantage of nature's bounty. Evidence discovered on the site shows that they cultivated cereals, grew grapes and apples, ate chickpeas, lentils and pistachio nuts, reared sheep and cattle, and hunted wild boar, goats and deer. They even kept pet dogs to guard their homes.

Urban life

Although Catal Hüyük is the oldest and largest example of an urban settlement, it does not resemble a town in the modern sense. The mudbrick houses were laid out in a large cluster and there were no streets – and no front doors. People entered their houses from the roof. Rooms were small, and their plaster walls were often decorated with paintings showing hunting or farming scenes. Catal Hüyük's residents were among the first people in the world to produce fabrics, wooden bowls and even mirrors. They also traded goods with other communities from miles around. Fertility symbols were important and they probably believed in some sort of life after death – the dead were buried beneath the floors of houses with objects they would have used in life, such as pots, beads and bracelets.

▲ This reconstruction of a group of houses in Catal Hüyük shows neat houses, closely packed together. There were no windows or proper streets, and people entered their houses through the roofs.

▼ This aerial view of what Catal Hüyük might have looked like shows the mudbrick houses packed tightly together. Surrounding the town was a fertile plain – very different from today – with wide areas of marshes that flooded easily, and areas inhabited by horses, deer and wild boar.

▲ At Newgrange there are several large stones intricately decorated with patterns such as these spirals. Above the doorway you can see the 'roof box' through which at midwinter the sun's rays shine along the passage.

Giant stones of western Europe

Eternal monuments to the dead or meeting places for the living? Astronomical calculators or celestial clocks? Boundary stones to mark land ownership or religious shrines to prepare people for the next life? Perhaps we shall never know for sure why prehistoric peoples throughout western Europe built their mysterious, giant stone monuments, thousands of which adorn the landscape. But we do know that their haunting power to fascinate has not diminished – even after 5,000 years.

The passage grave at Newgrange

The prehistoric stone structure at Newgrange in Ireland, built around 3000BCE, is one of the most famous in western Europe. The passage grave consists of a large stone and turf mound containing a passage which leads to a burial chamber. Like many other prehistoric stone arrangements, the whole structure at Newgrange is precisely aligned so that something special happens at a certain time of the year. At Newgrange, on the shortest day of the year (known as the winter solstice) the rising sun shines directly along the passage, illuminating the wall of the burial chamber.

The mystery

Each winter solstice, for a brief period of about 17 minutes, the dawn rays of the midwinter sun – in perfect alignment with the passage and the burial chamber – shine light into the darkness. This does not happen by chance. Human beings designed it to be so. Why? Does it symbolize that winter will soon give way to spring? Or something more – a belief that light and life will triumph over darkness and death? No written records exist to help us decide. That is the mystery of Newgrange.

◄ The 27 standing stones of the Ring of Brodgar in Orkney, Scotland, form part of a complex of ritual structures. Also on Orkney is a superbly preserved village of stone houses from the same period (3100–2500BCE).

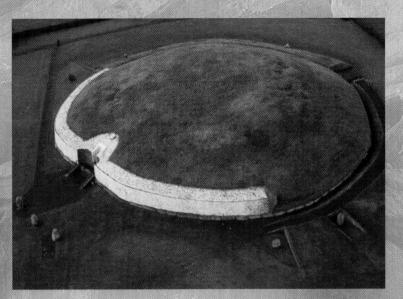

Eternally fascinating

These massive stones are also called megaliths – from the Greek words *mega*, meaning large, and *lithos*, meaning stone. People have always been fascinated by them, their locations, and why they were built. The stones were transported across large distances for no obvious practical purpose, so surely they must have had great importance in communities' ritual or religious life. It was only in the 1950s that archaeologists realized that they dated to between 3000 and 1500BCE. As new finds come to light, they are building up more of a picture of the people who lived with them.

The big questions

The megaliths may have been temples, places of ceremony or sacrifice, or giant calendars for recording the seasons. We can be sure that these monuments were built with life's big questions in mind – how we people fit into the pattern of the universe, who or what controls our lives, and what awaits us after death. Many were built to house the dead, and the importance of funeral rites was enormous. Objects unearthed in burial mounds suggest that people in these early societies believed that death was not the end of things but that it was part of a longer journey.

▲ The passage in the burial chamber at Newgrange, dazzlingly lit up by the midwinter sun, must have been an awesome sight for those who witnessed it in prehistoric times. Rediscovered in CE1699, it is still magnificent today.

► At Carnac in Brittany, France, there are stone alignments made up of 3,000 megaliths, stretching for several kilometres. They might have been used as a place of worship. They might also have been devices to track the changing patterns of the sky, in a society where climate and the seasons were important.

Harappa and Mohenjo-Daro

Near the cities of Lahore and Hyderabad in modern-day Pakistan stand the ruins of two of the earliest and greatest prehistoric brick cities, built along the Indus valley around 2700BCE. These cities were part of a major Bronze Age civilization. Forgotten and neglected for centuries, they were first excavated by archaeologists in the CE1920s.

▲ Some archaeologists have suggested that the ordered grid pattern of the streets and houses of the Indus valley cities (seen here at Mohenjo-Daro) is the earliest attempt at deliberate town planning. Excavations have revealed that almost every house was connected to sewers and a water supply.

Harappa
When archaeologists started to excavate the site at Harappa, they found the remains of a remarkable city. It had been built to a neat grid pattern, with houses at right angles to each other. In 1921, they unearthed evidence of a massive citadel (stronghold) that looked down on the residential quarters and which had contained public buildings such as workshops and a large grain store which, to the people of the city, served as a kind of central bank.

Cities of traders
The merchants of the Indus valley established links with surrounding peoples – even as far afield as modern-day Iraq – trading timber, precious stones, gold and ivory. In Harappa the goods were stored in warehouses, where archaeologists have discovered a number of clay seals. These would have identified a particular merchant. Terracotta models of distinctive two-wheeled carts have also been found, giving an indication of how goods were transported overland.

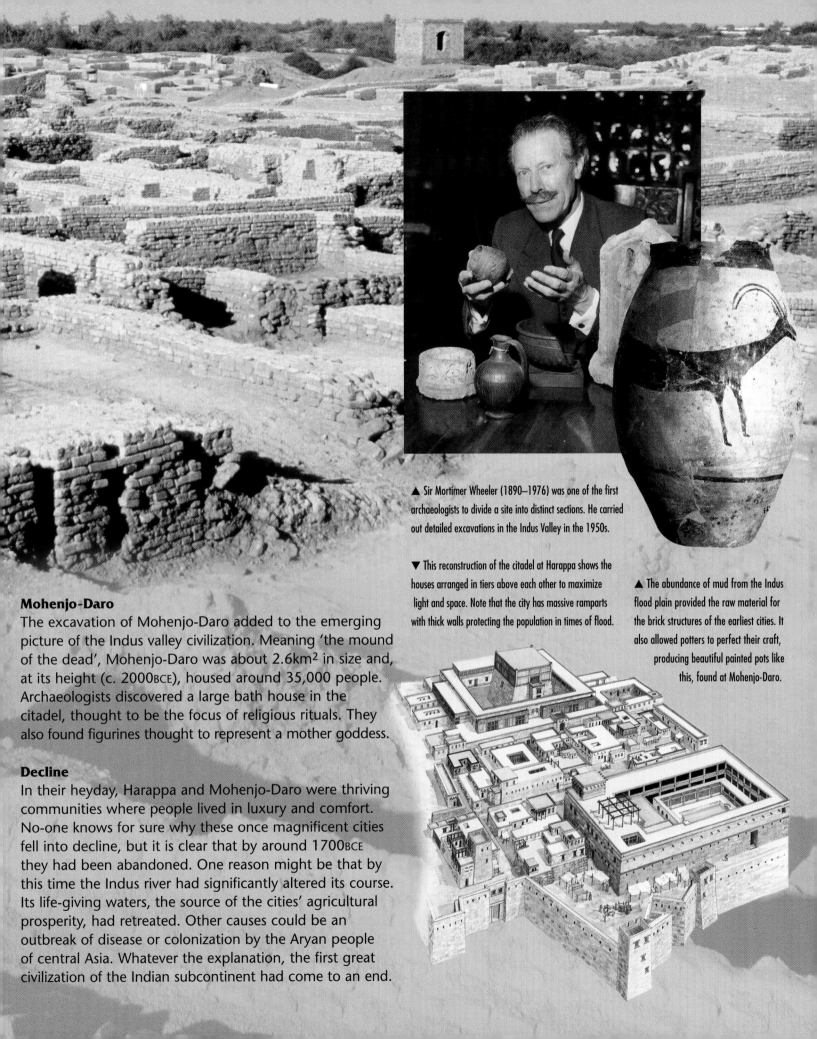

▲ Sir Mortimer Wheeler (1890–1976) was one of the first archaeologists to divide a site into distinct sections. He carried out detailed excavations in the Indus Valley in the 1950s.

▼ This reconstruction of the citadel at Harappa shows the houses arranged in tiers above each other to maximize light and space. Note that the city has massive ramparts with thick walls protecting the population in times of flood.

▲ The abundance of mud from the Indus flood plain provided the raw material for the brick structures of the earliest cities. It also allowed potters to perfect their craft, producing beautiful painted pots like this, found at Mohenjo-Daro.

Mohenjo-Daro

The excavation of Mohenjo-Daro added to the emerging picture of the Indus valley civilization. Meaning 'the mound of the dead', Mohenjo-Daro was about 2.6km² in size and, at its height (c. 2000BCE), housed around 35,000 people. Archaeologists discovered a large bath house in the citadel, thought to be the focus of religious rituals. They also found figurines thought to represent a mother goddess.

Decline

In their heyday, Harappa and Mohenjo-Daro were thriving communities where people lived in luxury and comfort. No-one knows for sure why these once magnificent cities fell into decline, but it is clear that by around 1700BCE they had been abandoned. One reason might be that by this time the Indus river had significantly altered its course. Its life-giving waters, the source of the cities' agricultural prosperity, had retreated. Other causes could be an outbreak of disease or colonization by the Aryan people of central Asia. Whatever the explanation, the first great civilization of the Indian subcontinent had come to an end.

▲ This ornate gold and silver double ring for holding oxen reins was found in the royal graves of Ur.

Ur and Babylon

Mesopotamia, in the 'Fertile Crescent' of land bounded by the rivers Tigris and Euphrates (in modern-day Iraq), has been called the cradle of civilization. It was here, around 5,000 years ago, that the Sumerians, Assyrians and Babylonians built great cities and laid the foundations of magnificent civilizations. Archaeologists have built a fascinating picture of these places.

The Sumerian city of Ur

Ur, one of the oldest cities of Mesopotamia, was at its height from 2100 to 2000BCE. Writing was first developed there. Its remains were discovered in CE1854, when archaeologists found a massive earth and brick mound at the site. Later excavations revealed a huge step-sided pyramid, known as a ziggurat. This was the centrepiece of the ancient city and was used mainly for worship. At the top was a temple, while at lower levels there were rooms for animal sacrifice and for the preparation of other offerings to the gods.

The royal graves

In 1926, at a cemetery where the ancient kings and queens had been buried, archaeologists discovered a vast array of precious objects – from golden helmets and shields to elaborate musical instruments made in the shape of animals. The graves also contained a grim secret. A living procession of soldiers, musicians and servants had accompanied the royal corpses into the tomb. Each had carried a deadly poison which they would drink once inside, ready to accompany their rulers into eternity.

◄ With the discovery of the royal graves at Ur, a wealth of evidence of a rich and sophisticated civilization came to light. Treasures included this necklace worn by Queen Pu-abi of Ur (died c. 2500BCE). She was buried in all her finery, accompanied by 25 attendants who were buried and went to their death alongside her.

The rise of Babylon

Over the centuries, Ur was gradually overshadowed in Mesopotamia by the city of Babylon, at its height under King Nebuchadnezzar (ruled 605–562BCE). He fortified the city with massive ramparts and built an elaborate blue glazed brick gate, dedicated to Ishtar, goddess of love. Inside the city walls was the Temple of Marduk, a vast ziggurat modelled on the one at Ur. The king ordered it to be built even higher than the one at Ur, so that it would be a visible symbol of the city's wealth and power

The Hanging Gardens

Archaeologists have unearthed evidence of glazed bricks used for Babylon's Ishtar Gate, and a reconstruction of it has been built in the Pergamon Museum, Berlin, Germany, complete with decorations based on animals and mythical beasts. The city's most famous structure, however, was a vast artificial mountain displaying a stunning collection of exotic plants, shrubs and flowers. The Hanging Gardens of Babylon were one of the seven wonders of the ancient world. They have captured people's imagination ever since, although to this day no actual remains have been found.

▼ Nebuchadnezzar ordered the Temple of Marduk
to be so vast that it would 'reach up to heaven'.
Many people think that this could have been the
origin of the biblical legend of the Tower of Babel,
a tower that was built to try to reach heaven.

▲ The blue Ishtar Gate is the only monument from
Babylon which has well-preserved remains. Behind it
in this artist's reconstruction is the impressive Temple
of Marduk. Step-sided ziggurats such as this were a
characteristic feature of the Mesopotamian landscape
and symbolized the link between heaven and earth.
Behind it are the magnificent Hanging Gardens.

The palace at Knossos

Legend tells us that many thousands of years ago, on the Mediterranean island we know today as Crete, there lived a cruel tyrant, King Minos. His fabulous palace contained an underground maze, a labyrinth guarded by a terrible monster known as the Minotaur, who was half man and half bull. Many stories were told about Minos, the Minotaur and the labyrinth. But was it ever more than just a story? Could the palace really have existed, and the myths have had a basis in historical fact? A 19th-century English archaeologist was convinced that it could.

▲ Sir Arthur Evans was the first to excavate the palace of Knossos. He coined the term 'Minoan' to describe the rich civilization he unearthed.

Myth into fact

In CE1899, the archaeologist Arthur Evans (1851–1941) bought a plot of land in the town of Knossos and began excavations. He discovered the remains of an ornate palace with a maze of corridors and courtyards – and everywhere, in mosaics, frescoes and statues, images of bulls. The story of the labyrinth was written down around 1000BCE, but the archaeological evidence suggested that the palace had been built at least a thousand years earlier. Could a real palace with a network of corridors, with people who revered bulls and enjoyed bull fighting, have inspired a story that was embellished down the generations? Evans thought so.

◄ Bulls were a symbol of male power and fertility in many civilizations of this time. This bull-shaped *rhyton* (ritual pouring vessel, used to pour liquids as part of a religious ceremony), comes from Mycenae, the Mediterranean civilization that was to destroy Knossos.

A luxurious life

Evans discovered evidence of a fabulous palace. Its courtyards offered cool spaces where, in summer, people could escape the fierce heat. In winter, underfloor heating kept the palace warm. Sunken baths, running water and lush gardens all added to the splendour. But it was more than just a royal palace. It was a whole town in miniature, with store rooms, temples, workshops – everything to support a Bronze Age civilization 4,000 years ago.

Minoan civilization

The Minoan civilization was the first great European civilization. Its position at the centre of the Mediterranean trade routes was crucial to its success. But the island's wealth attracted the envy of another palace civilization, based in Mycenae, to the north-west. From the 15th century BCE, Mycenean warriors began to invade and colonize Crete, signalling the beginning of the end of the Minoan way of life.

▲ The bull was given an honoured place in society and depicted on everything from pottery to wall paintings. There were elaborate games involving young athletes leaping over the bulls' horns and doing handstands on the bulls' backs as the animals charged towards them.

▶ Parts of the ancient palace at Knossos were reconstructed by Evans and his team. Although undoubtedly beautiful they were criticized by some for using modern materials such as reinforced concrete for the supporting pillars. This is the Grand Staircase, with the Royal Guardroom in the background.

The tomb of Tutankhamun

The civilization of the ancient Egyptians lasted for over 2,000 years, ending around 1000BCE. They were ruled by pharaohs (kings) and the country is dotted with vast pyramids and elaborate royal tombs, built as monuments to the dead pharaohs and filled with objects for their journey through the afterlife. One tomb is that of the boy-king Tutankhamun (died c. 1400BCE). He reigned for just a short time but his tomb, when opened, revealed the most spectacular collection of treasures the world had ever seen.

A preoccupation with death

The Egyptians believed that death was just the next stage in a person's life. They thought that they could only be reborn, and live forever, if their bodies were preserved. Egyptians preserved their dead as mummies, and placed them in sarcophagi (stone coffins). Royal mummies were entombed in burial chambers beneath the desert, often topped by imposing pyramids which symbolized stairways to the stars.

The tombs

The tombs of the Egyptian pharaohs were filled with objects thought to be of use in the afterlife. In many cases, grave robbers over the years have looted the tombs and stolen the riches they contain. For many years archaeologists have sought to discover and put on public display artefacts that tell us more about the civilization of ancient Egypt. Howard Carter (1874–1939) was just such a man.

pharaoh's belongings

burial chamber

treasure room and shrine

▲ Tutankhamun's tomb as seen by Howard Carter.

A discovery waiting to happen

All over Egypt there are tombs, some of which have yet to reveal their secrets. One is that of Hatshepsut, one of the few female pharaohs. She ruled for 15 years until her death in 1458BCE, in place of her nephew, Tuthmosis III (died 1426BCE), who was too young to rule. After her death, Tuthmosis tried to erase her from history by attacking monuments to her and removing her name from written records. But he left her tomb alone and it remained intact for centuries, leaving today's archaeologists with yet more mysteries to solve.

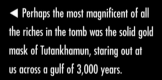

◄ Perhaps the most magnificent of all the riches in the tomb was the solid gold mask of Tutankhamun, staring out at us across a gulf of 3,000 years.

▲ The tomb was a jumble of the most amazing artefacts – strange and beguiling objects from an ancient civilization. The dry atmosphere meant that even such things as nuts, dried fruits and funeral flowers had been preserved.

The tomb of Tutankhamun

On 26 November 1922, Carter was on the brink of one of the most exciting discoveries any archaeologist has ever made. He was convinced he was at the outside of the walled-up tomb of Tutankhamun. He lit a candle and made a hole in the wall. The dead air that had last been breathed by the pharaoh's servants made the flame flicker, but when his eyes had adjusted to the light he looked on the most wonderful things he had ever seen – chests, statues, musical instruments, wine jars, clothes, games, mummies, jewels, swords, daggers and much, much more. Everyday objects for a pharaoh; priceless treasures for the modern world.

▲ Hatshepsut's tomb in the Valley of the Kings was discovered by Howard Carter in 1916. In his diaries he describes how he surprised tomb robbers at work in the entrance and chased them away. The tomb is still being excavated by archaeologists today and they are finding new things all the time.

The Acropolis at Athens

The Acropolis, the citadel that once contained some of the most impressive structures the world has ever seen, dominates the Greek city of Athens. Its ruins are a visible reminder of the achievements of a vanished society which laid the foundations of western civilization. The remains are a history in stone of a culture which gave the world politics, mathematics, drama, philosophy and democracy. It was on the Acropolis that these words took practical shape, contributing to a society which prized beauty, truth and order above all else.

▲ These figures, called Caryatids, support part of the porch of the Erechtheum, a temple on the Acropolis built in honour of the goddess Athene, the god Poseidon and Erechtheus, legendary king of Athens.

▶ The Parthenon dominates the Acropolis. It has had many uses – it became a Christian shrine in the 5th century CE and a mosque in the 15th century. Later, it was used as a gunpowder store, and was largely destroyed after an explosion in CE1687.

Fortress and shrine

The Acropolis was a natural fortress in times of war and the place in which Athenians conducted their social, political and religious lives in times of peace. Archaeologists have uncovered evidence that it had been in continuous use as a settlement or shrine since before 650BCE. During the Classical period (460–330BCE), three temples were built on the ruins of earlier ones. The most important is the Parthenon – built by the Athenian statesman Pericles (c. 495–429BCE) and dedicated to the city's protecting spirit, the goddess Athene.

The Parthenon

Built from the finest marble and originally brightly painted, the Parthenon became the emblem of classical Greek civilization. Running around the top was a carved frieze depicting a procession which was part of a great four-yearly festival in honour of Athene. By studying its wealth of detail, archaeologists can piece together a picture of life, worship and celebration in Greece in the 5th century BCE.

Beyond Athens

There were many other shrines to the gods and goddesses of ancient Greece. One of the most important was the shrine to Apollo, 'the bright one', at Delphi. Excavations began in CE1893 and the artefacts that were unearthed showed how the Greeks worshipped Apollo as the light of reason and order – as opposed to the dark of chaos and ignorance. They also believed Delphi to be at the centre or 'navel' of the world. Priestesses there foretold the future in riddles. Modern geological examination has suggested they may have made their predictions while in a trance-like state thanks to hallucinogenic gases escaping from the rocks.

▼ Parts of the Parthenon frieze were removed by Lord Elgin (1766–1841) in the 19th century, and sold to the British Museum in London, England, where they have remained for over 200 years. The Greek government has repeatedly asked for their return and hopes one day to house them near the Acropolis.

The terracotta army

▲ Qin Shi Huangdi was a ruthless emperor who imposed his authority violently. Here he is shown executing scholars.

For over 2,000 years, the plains around Mount Li, near present-day Xi'an in China, were hiding an astonishing secret. In 1974, by chance, the secret came to light. What emerged captured the imagination of the world. Peasants digging wells had found fragments of life-sized terracotta figures of soldiers. Archaeologists were intrigued and started excavating the site. There, in a series of ancient trenches which had lain undisturbed since 200BCE, was a terracotta army of 7,500 full size warriors, horses and chariots.

Standing guard

The statues at Mount Li were there to protect China's first emperor, Qin Shi Huangdi (259–210BCE), on his journey through the afterlife. Qin Shi Huangdi ruled his people with a rod of iron and he was greatly feared. Even dropping litter in his capital city, Luoyang, could be punished by flogging or by a heavy fine. Yet under his rule the peasants were largely well-off, thanks to his reforms.

▲ In a field near Xi'an in north-central China stands the burial mound of the emperor. It is rumoured to contain fabulous treasures – but also booby traps for those who dare to enter.

◄ Figures in the terracotta army are astonishingly life-like and look as if they really are ready to fight to defend the dead emperor. They were painted in the colours of their platoons, but over time the colours faded to an ash grey.

The emperor's achievements

During his reign, Qin Shi Huangdi improved the agricultural and road systems, and standardized both the currency and the writing system. His prosperous empire was often targeted for attack – particularly on its northern frontier – by tribes of nomads. These enemies had no permanent settlements to invade and destroy, so they were impossible to defeat. Instead they had to be kept out. Qin Shi Huangdi famously ordered the construction of the Great Wall of China, a huge defensive barrier. When completed centuries later, the wall stretched across the entire northern border of the empire, for almost 2,500km.

▶ Chinese archaeologists slowly and painstakingly uncover a row of statues that had been hidden for over 2,000 years. They take great care not to damage the statues as they clear away their covering of earth.

Attention to detail

Careful study of the statues showed that no two were the same. Each had been sculpted from life and showed, in breathtaking detail, what the imperial army of the time would have looked like. The heads and bodies of the soldiers were hollow but their legs were solid to bear the weight. Just as they had served the emperor in life, so they guarded his tomb and were believed to protect him in death. For this they had been armed with real weapons. Amazingly, when Chinese archaeologists examined them they found that many of the blades were still sharp enough to cut through flesh.

The riddle of the tomb

Although the burial pits with their model army have been excavated, these are just part of a vast necropolis (elaborate 'city of the dead') inside Mount Li which also includes a palace and temple. The emperor's tomb itself has so far been left untouched. There are rumours that it contains fabulous treasures – rivers of mercury, gold and silver statues, ornaments made of jade and precious stones and much more. But there are also rumours that within the tomb lie great dangers – lethal booby traps and crossbows primed 2,000 years ago, aimed and ready to fire at anyone bold enough to disturb the great ruler's final earthly resting place.

▶ Qin Shi Huangdi began preparing for his life in the afterworld long before his death in 210BCE. Historical sources tell us that over 700,000 men were conscripted to build the burial mound. Surrounding the tomb are at least four large pits containing terracotta warriors. Pit number one, shown here, contains 3,200 soldiers. The figures were modelled on the imperial army and include cavalrymen, infantrymen, archers and charioteers.

Pompeii

▲ The minutest details of Pompeiian life remain, from these eggs and eggshells to loaves of bread probably baked on the day of the eruption and carbonised in the heat.

For the people of the Roman city of Pompeii, 24 August CE79 began like any other day. As they awoke, none could have known that their lives would soon be at an end, and the city buried under volcanic ash. Only hours later, Vesuvius erupted, firing molten lava and rock that rained down on the city. The terrified inhabitants were buried where they fell, suffocated by the heat. But the layers of ash that shrouded the city also preserved it, fixing it in time for over 1,700 years.

Opening the time capsule

The systematic excavation of Pompeii and nearby Herculaneum (which suffered a similar fate) was begun around CE1860. Colourful wall paintings which came to light from beneath the dust show the luxury and grace enjoyed by the well-to-do Roman citizens. They shopped from market stalls overflowing with fruit, vegetables and fish; they wore fine fabrics; they lived in stylish houses, many of them built around an elegant central courtyard.

Entertainment

The public buildings that have been excavated in Pompeii show that the people had a passion for public spectacles and entertainments of every kind. In the *paelestra* or gymnasium, for example, they could watch sporting competitions, while in the nearby amphitheatre there were bloody contests between gladiators and wild beasts. They could watch plays in the theatre or go to the baths where they could gossip about the details of their lives.

▼ Ruins such as those of the House of the Faun let us see inside the actual homes of the Pompeiians. In the foreground is an elaborate marble floor.

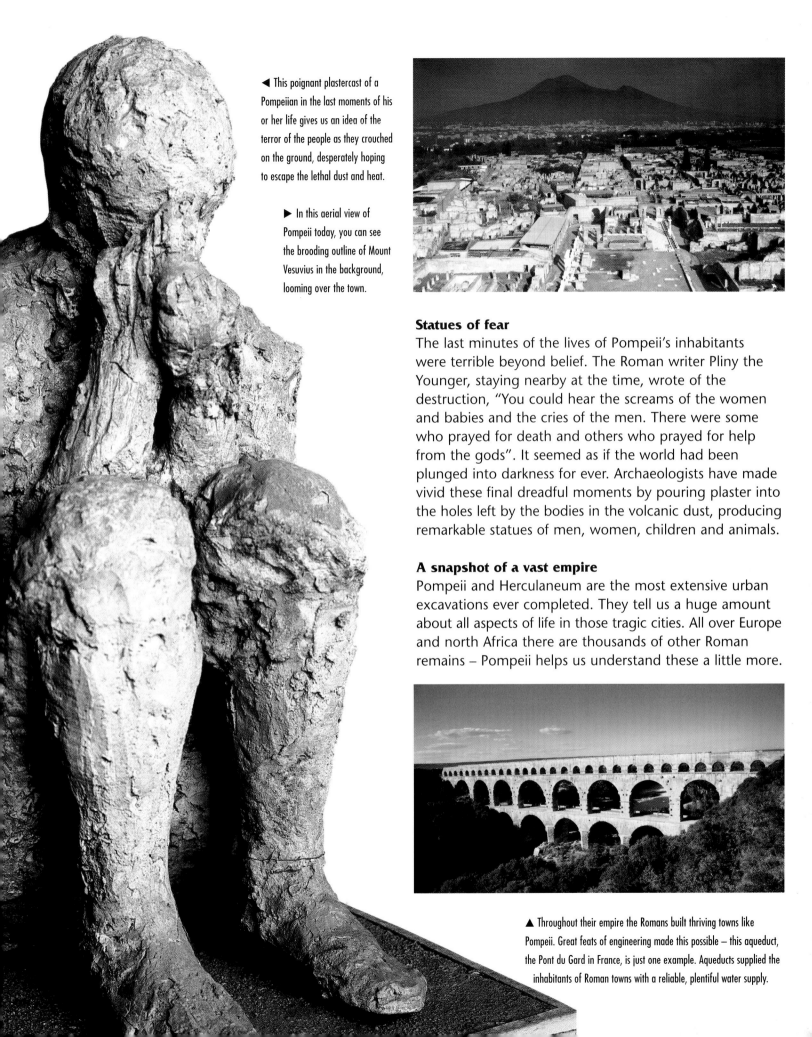

◄ This poignant plastercast of a Pompeiian in the last moments of his or her life gives us an idea of the terror of the people as they crouched on the ground, desperately hoping to escape the lethal dust and heat.

► In this aerial view of Pompeii today, you can see the brooding outline of Mount Vesuvius in the background, looming over the town.

Statues of fear

The last minutes of the lives of Pompeii's inhabitants were terrible beyond belief. The Roman writer Pliny the Younger, staying nearby at the time, wrote of the destruction, "You could hear the screams of the women and babies and the cries of the men. There were some who prayed for death and others who prayed for help from the gods". It seemed as if the world had been plunged into darkness for ever. Archaeologists have made vivid these final dreadful moments by pouring plaster into the holes left by the bodies in the volcanic dust, producing remarkable statues of men, women, children and animals.

A snapshot of a vast empire

Pompeii and Herculaneum are the most extensive urban excavations ever completed. They tell us a huge amount about all aspects of life in those tragic cities. All over Europe and north Africa there are thousands of other Roman remains – Pompeii helps us understand these a little more.

▲ Throughout their empire the Romans built thriving towns like Pompeii. Great feats of engineering made this possible – this aqueduct, the Pont du Gard in France, is just one example. Aqueducts supplied the inhabitants of Roman towns with a reliable, plentiful water supply.

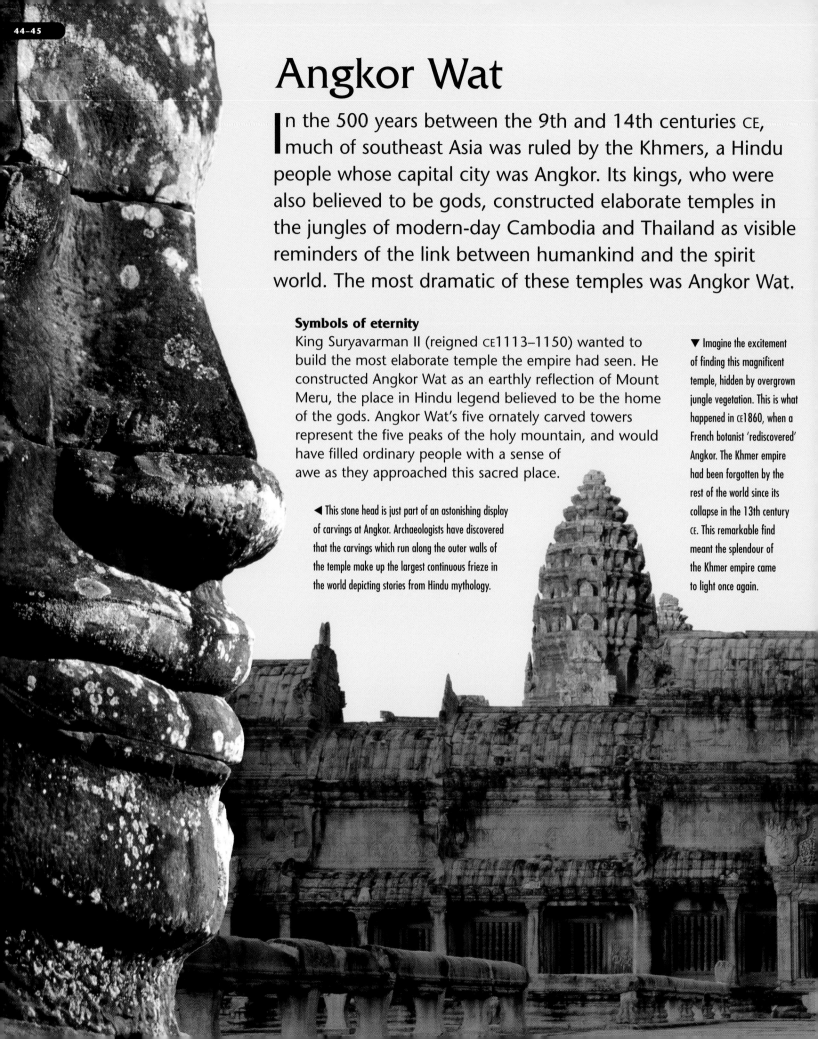

Angkor Wat

In the 500 years between the 9th and 14th centuries CE, much of southeast Asia was ruled by the Khmers, a Hindu people whose capital city was Angkor. Its kings, who were also believed to be gods, constructed elaborate temples in the jungles of modern-day Cambodia and Thailand as visible reminders of the link between humankind and the spirit world. The most dramatic of these temples was Angkor Wat.

Symbols of eternity

King Suryavarman II (reigned CE1113–1150) wanted to build the most elaborate temple the empire had seen. He constructed Angkor Wat as an earthly reflection of Mount Meru, the place in Hindu legend believed to be the home of the gods. Angkor Wat's five ornately carved towers represent the five peaks of the holy mountain, and would have filled ordinary people with a sense of awe as they approached this sacred place.

◄ This stone head is just part of an astonishing display of carvings at Angkor. Archaeologists have discovered that the carvings which run along the outer walls of the temple make up the largest continuous frieze in the world depicting stories from Hindu mythology.

▼ Imagine the excitement of finding this magnificent temple, hidden by overgrown jungle vegetation. This is what happened in CE1860, when a French botanist 'rediscovered' Angkor. The Khmer empire had been forgotten by the rest of the world since its collapse in the 13th century CE. This remarkable find meant the splendour of the Khmer empire came to light once again.

A model of the universe

The city of Angkor was criss-crossed by a complex network of irrigation channels, which supplied drinking water to the people and watered the surrounding rice fields. The main compound was surrounded by a giant moat and approached by a causeway, whose balustrades were carved in the form of serpents representing the fertility of the universe. The canal system was designed to be practical and to reflect the religious belief that Mount Meru was surrounded by a vast ocean. Archaeologists have taken precise measurements of the temple and shown that it was built to symbolize the movements of the sun and moon. As such, Angkor Wat is modelled on the universe itself.

▲ Angkor Wat is a huge temple complex, surrounded by walls and a moat 180m wide and 4km long. The temple is modelled on the universe itself and represents, in fixed stone, the movement of the heavens. The inner holy sanctum and its five ornate central towers are clearly visible in this aerial view.

Everyday life

The temple carvings also tell us a lot about the everyday lives of the Khmer people. They show them at work and at play, preparing food, hunting or tending their animals. Evidence from the site shows that the central complex was used as a religious and administrative headquarters, housing the royal family and the court. Peasants lived in the fields beyond, in bamboo huts built on stilts. They would have supported their families on livestock reared on their domestic plots.

A people at war

The Khmers' civilization came at a price. Their supremacy in the region depended on force of arms, and the temple carvings show kings and soldiers going into battle on elephants equipped for fighting. Their tusks were armed with sharp metal points designed to inflict maximum damage on the enemy at the same time as bowmen sitting on the elephants' backs would unleash a lethal volley of arrows onto the opposing army. These vivid scenes of battle carved onto the silent stone are all that remain of a once powerful empire.

Cahokia

One thousand years ago, hunters travelling along what we now know as America's central Mississippi river valley would have come across an extraordinary sight. Rising up from the flat plains all around was a collection of neatly arranged timber and mud houses with a giant, 30m-tall mound towering above the centre. To the weary travellers it would have looked like a modern-day metropolis – which, in its way, it was.

▲ Before the Mississippian culture developed, an earlier native American culture called the Hopewell culture flourished in the region, between 200BCE and CE500. This Hopewell stone ornament has a distinctive hand symbol.

A trading people

Cahokia was the most sophisticated prehistoric settlement north of Mexico and, at its height (around CE1100–1250), it was home to between 10,000 and 20,000 people. Merchants travelling far and wide helped to spread the so-called Mississippian culture over a vast area from the Gulf coast in the south to the Great Lakes in the north, and the Atlantic coast in the east to what is now Oklahoma in the west.

Daily life

In its heyday, Cahokia teemed with life. Men and women farmed the surrounding land, growing pumpkins, sunflowers and corn, while others fished and hunted to provide the community with food. When not at work, they enjoyed singing and dancing and, as archaeological evidence has shown, playing dice games.

The settlement was ruled by a chief who was believed to be the brother of the sun and gifted with spiritual power. Beneath him were members of his family. Trusted friends also exercised authority. Together these people formed an elite (superior) class separate from the ordinary people.

The great stockade

At the heart of the settlement was a 3km-long wooden stockade (protective fence). For a long time, archaeologists thought this performed a purely social function, screening off the elite and well-to-do from everyone else. Examination has shown that it was primarily used as a defensive structure to protect the settlement if attacked.

▲ Great Serpent Mound in Ohio is the finest of America's so-called effigy mounds, built around 2,000 years ago. No skeletons have been found there, suggesting that it was not a burial place but a ritual structure. The ripples in the snake's back are aligned with the rays of the sun at key times of the year.

The mounds

The most distinctive feature of the Cahokia settlement is its series of over a hundred earth mounds. The exact purpose of these is not clear, though some were used for burial purposes and others to support houses raised up off the ground. The largest mound, known as Monk's Mound, is situated at the heart of the settlement and towering above it. At the top, sacred fires burned day and night in honour of the gods. There are other, smaller mound settlements in the area. At Moundville, Alabama, the burial mounds have been found to be particularly rich in artefacts.

▼ Cahokia's houses were arranged in rows around an open plaza (square). They had pitched roofs topped with magnificent carved animal heads. In its day, the settlement was one of the continent's great urban centres. It contained not only ordinary homes but structures for communal use, such as meeting halls, grain stores and sauna-like sweat lodges.

Kingdoms in west Africa

Visitors to the bustling industrial town of Ife in Nigeria may be unaware of a hidden city beneath their feet. For hundreds of years it has been slowly slipping out of sight, buried under successive layers of new building. But if the ruins of that ancient city could speak, they would tell tales of a great civilization that flourished for over three centuries from the 12th century CE. Ife and nearby Benin were the centres of important forest kingdoms in western Africa at this time. These sites are rich in artefacts which allows the past to speak to us today.

▲ Nature moves swiftly to swallow up evidence of the past. Here the ruins of the ancient city of Benin and its 13th century CE fortifications have been overgrown by dense vegetation.

A religious capital

Ife was the capital of the Yoruba kingdom, the spiritual homeland of a nation whose rulers were believed to be gods. According to tradition, it was founded in around CE1300 by Oduduwa, the first mythological oni or king of Ife. When a king died, exquisitely crafted masks bearing his likeness were cast out of iron, copper or bronze, and carried aloft by the people who believed he would continue to help them overcome difficulties in their lives. Many of these beautiful and mysterious artefacts survive today.

Daily life

The people of Ife and Benin made their living herding cattle and growing crops in the fertile grasslands of western Africa. Oil from cultivated palms was used not only for cooking but also for offering to Ogun, the warrior god of metalworking. Shrines to Ogun have been discovered in the royal palace at Ife, together with masks depicting the trickster spirit Eshu, the gods' messenger. The sculptures of kings, queens, gods and goddesses show these kingdoms had a complex, highly developed religious and artistic culture.

▶ When Portuguese explorers arrived in west Africa in the 15th century CE, Ife was in decline, eclipsed by the neighbouring kingdoms of Benin and Oyo. Masks like this, from Benin, depicted gods and kings, and were an expression of the power and mystery of the royal court. They were sometimes placed on altars during religious rituals or worn as part of court ceremonials.

◀ In this bronze plaque, discovered in the royal palace at Benin, the oba or king is shown with two warriors bearing lances at his side. The kingship of Benin was related to that of Ife – the oba of Benin is traditionally thought to be a descendant of Oduduwa, the founder of Ife. Both cities had elaborate royal palaces and shrines.

▲ Gertrude Caton-Thompson (CE1888–1985) began excavations at Great Zimbabwe in 1929. She proved that this had been a major site of African culture in the 11th to 14th centuries CE.

Great Zimbabwe

At the same time, hundreds of kilometres to the southeast of Ife and Benin there was another remarkable civilization which has fascinated archaeologists. The ruins of Great Zimbabwe, a massive stone enclosure or 'zimbabwe' which once housed a palace city, were systematically excavated in the early 20th century by the British archaeologist Gertrude Caton-Thompson. At the time, many Europeans thought that this African culture had been influenced by European, especially Portuguese, explorers and travellers. Her research on objects she excavated at the site showed otherwise.

▲ The stone-walled enclosure of Great Zimbabwe is the largest and most impressive of several similar enclosures in southeast Africa. For many years the question of who built it remained a mystery. It is now thought to have been built by the Shona people.

The Aztecs' great temple

▲ The Aztecs recorded their history not in writing as we know it but in a system of pictures, in books called codices. Many show the Templo Mayor and the ritual sacrifices performed there.

The Aztecs settled in present-day Mexico in the 12th century CE, following the collapse of the earlier Toltec civilization. In the early 14th century they founded the city of Tenochtitlan, built on an island in a lake. Within 400 years they had conquered many peoples and built up a rich, mighty and fearsome empire. At the centre of their empire was Tenochtitlan. At the centre of the city, and the heart of city life, was the Aztecs' great temple, the Templo Mayor.

The sacred city

The heart of Tenochtitlan was its sacred plaza, an area of temples and pyramids used for worshipping the gods of rain, fire, wind, sun and war. Dominating the plaza was the Templo Mayor, topped by two temples – to the rain god Tlaloc and the sun god Huitzilopochtli. The Aztecs believed that, every night, Huitzilopochtli left the sky and did battle with the forces of the night. If he was killed, then never again would the sun rise. So, each night, he had to be strengthened – with blood from human sacrifice.

◀ This incense burner is in the form of the rain god Tlaloc. In an agricultural society which relied on sunshine and rainfall to ripen its crops, worship of gods of the elements was very important.

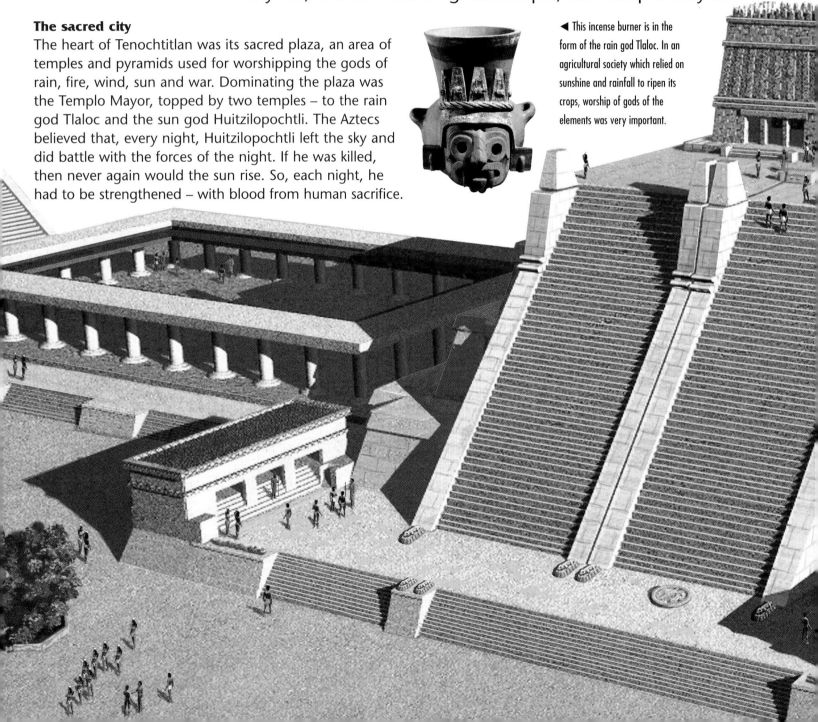

Rise and fall

Rumours of Tenochtitlan's wealth spread far and wide. Stories were told of its markets, harvests, jewellery and ornaments. In CF1519, these tales of riches attracted the Spanish conquistador (soldier-adventurer) Hernando Cortez (1485–1547). What he and his small army saw as they approached the city took their breath away – a dazzling vista of buildings surrounded by a clear blue lake. For a time, Cortez and the Aztec emperor, Montezuma II (1480–1520), got on well enough. But later the strangers laid siege to Tenochtitlan, plundered as much treasure as they could and finally demolished the city. Cortez established his own capital, Mexico City, on the same site.

▶ This picture shows the outline of the Templo Mayor laid over the top of a view of Mexico City as it is today. For many years it was generally believed that the Spanish had built their cathedral over the top of the site of the temple when they demolished the Aztec city of Tenochtitlan. But it was discovered buried beneath the city, and just next to the Metropolitan Cathedral, in 1978.

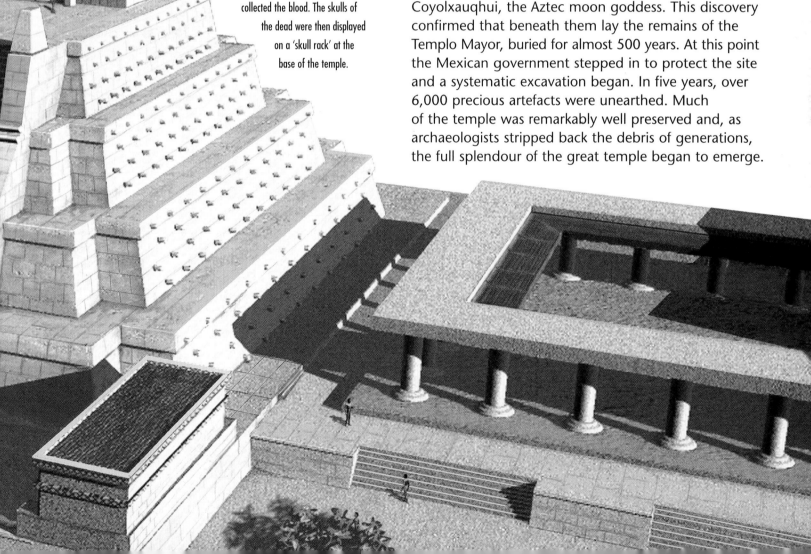

◀ On top of the Templo Mayor, the temple of Tlaloc is on the left and that of Huitzilopochtli on the right. The Aztecs' belief system demanded a constant supply of human sacrifices, including the nightly sacrifice to Huitzilopochtli. Often captured in war, the victims would be hacked to death with ritual daggers and their hearts, still beating, offered to the god. Special containers collected the blood. The skulls of the dead were then displayed on a 'skull rack' at the base of the temple.

Unearthing the great temple

Workers digging tunnels for a metro line in Mexico City in 1978 found something unusual – a stone disc with carvings depicting the dismembered body of a woman. Archaeologists identified it as a representation of Coyolxauqhui, the Aztec moon goddess. This discovery confirmed that beneath them lay the remains of the Templo Mayor, buried for almost 500 years. At this point the Mexican government stepped in to protect the site and a systematic excavation began. In five years, over 6,000 precious artefacts were unearthed. Much of the temple was remarkably well preserved and, as archaeologists stripped back the debris of generations, the full splendour of the great temple began to emerge.

The warship *Mary Rose*

On 11 October 1982, over 60 million people gathered around their television sets to witness an exciting archaeological event. Live pictures were being broadcast of an amazing and historic underwater salvage operation – the raising of part of a 16th-century CE English warship, that had lain on the sea floor for over 400 years since it sank in the summer of CE1545. The thrilling moment when a long-hidden artefact came to light was shared by an audience worldwide as the *Mary Rose* emerged from the deep.

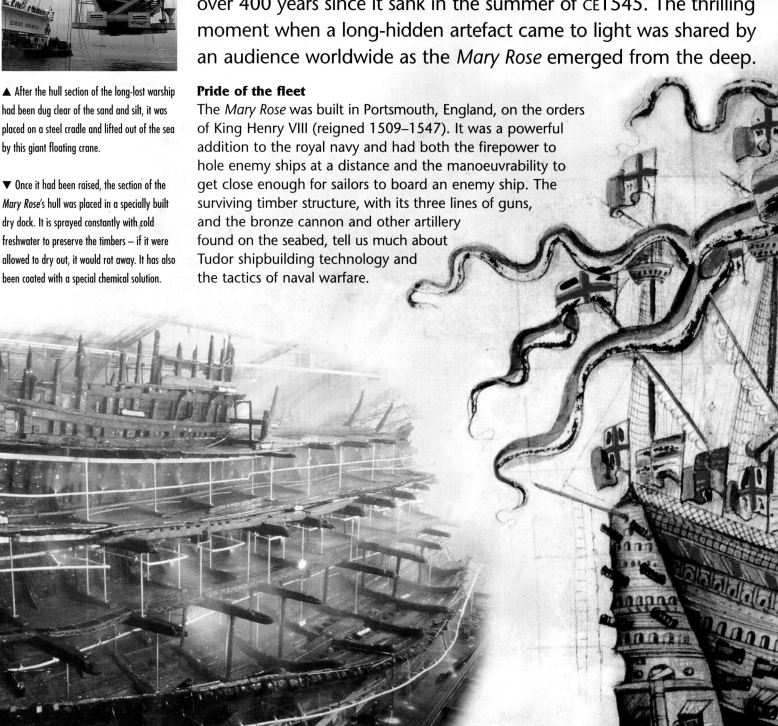

▲ After the hull section of the long-lost warship had been dug clear of the sand and silt, it was placed on a steel cradle and lifted out of the sea by this giant floating crane.

▼ Once it had been raised, the section of the *Mary Rose*'s hull was placed in a specially built dry dock. It is sprayed constantly with cold freshwater to preserve the timbers – if it were allowed to dry out, it would rot away. It has also been coated with a special chemical solution.

Pride of the fleet

The *Mary Rose* was built in Portsmouth, England, on the orders of King Henry VIII (reigned 1509–1547). It was a powerful addition to the royal navy and had both the firepower to hole enemy ships at a distance and the manoeuvrability to get close enough for sailors to board an enemy ship. The surviving timber structure, with its three lines of guns, and the bronze cannon and other artillery found on the seabed, tell us much about Tudor shipbuilding technology and the tactics of naval warfare.

Rediscovery

We know from historical records that the *Mary Rose* sank in the Solent, a stretch of water off Portsmouth harbour. But its exact location remained a mystery until 1971, when the shattered hull section was discovered on the seabed. Over the next ten years, archaeologists carried out underwater excavations to remove the silt from the wreck and to expose the ship's timbers. Specially-trained volunteers carried out thousands of dives. They also retrieved objects that had been used by the ship's crew – including personal possessions such as a whistle, rosary and comb.

▼ This idealized contemporary painting of the *Mary Rose* suggests the pride and admiration it inspired. When it sank, however, it was outdated and worn. It was an easy target for French warships – though some evidence suggests that unseaworthiness was the cause of its sinking.

▲ Underwater archaeology can be very difficult, but often leads to discoveries of great wealth or importance. This diver has recovered clay jars from the Glass Wreck, a ship that sank off the coast of Turkey in the 11th century CE with more than 200 pieces of glassware on board.

Raising the *Mary Rose*

Soon after the wreck had been found, engineers decided that it could be brought to the surface. Underwater archaeologists carried out a series of precise measurements to enable the engineers to build a special steel cradle onto which the hull could be transferred. A huge floating crane was used to lift the wreck clear of the sea floor and onto the cradle. Then both cradle and hull were lifted out of the sea.

The final clue?

In 2003, archaeologists diving close to where the ship had been discovered found a 5m-long piece of wood which they believe is the front section of the ship's keel. If tests show that the age and condition of the wood match those of the hull then the final piece of the ship will have been found. Archaeologists will have a complete cross-section of a Tudor warship.

▲ The French Emperor Napoleon (CE1769–1821) is pictured leading some of his army. Archaeologists have found evidence along the route of his retreat from Russia back to France that give us clues to the hardship faced by his soldiers.

Battlefield archaeology

Battlefields can be revealing places. Weapons and ammunition, uniforms and armour unearthed many years after their use paint a vivid picture of the realities of fighting. Eyewitness accounts and other historical records may tell us contradictory stories about a battle. How can we start to piece together a true picture? Often archaeology can help, as we turn to the battlefield itself to see what secrets it contains.

Into battle

On the afternoon of 25 June CE1876, the banks of the Little Bighorn river in Montana, USA, were baked dry by the sweltering sun. By nightfall, they had witnessed dramatic and bloody scenes of combat. It was here that General Custer (1839–1876) of the USA's 7th Cavalry had led his men into battle for the last time. It was the Battle of Little Bighorn, widely known as Custer's Last Stand.

A last stand?

This confrontation was part of a series of battles in the 1860s and 1870s between the American army and the armies of native American peoples, clashing as settlers moved into the natives' traditional homelands. In 1983, an extensive survey of the battlefield at Little Bighorn was carried out after an accidental fire had unexpectedly cleared the ground. Over 2,000 artefacts from the battle were discovered, from cartridge cases and bullets to human remains.

◀ General George Armstrong Custer has been portrayed as a great American hero, but archaeological evidence suggests that his expertise on the field of battle was limited.

The weapons' story

Archaeologists worked out, from the distribution of the shells, analysis of the weapons and the relative positions of the bodies, where individual weapons had been fired and where soldiers had moved on the battlefield. This showed that Custer's men did not face the enemy army in one dramatic last stand, but actually fled their attackers.

A lost army

Archaeology is constantly telling us more about past battles. In 2002, in Vilnius, Lithuania, builders discovered hundreds of skeletons buried in what appeared to be a mass grave. Examination showed that they dated from the early 19th century. Scraps of uniform, metal buttons and medals dated the grave more precisely. Here were the physical remains of part of Napoleon's lost army.

Napoleon, the French emperor, had by 1812 conquered much of Europe. That year he planned to conquer Russia. The plan was not a success and the army had to retreat – just as winter was setting in. Exhaustion, cold and starvation killed many of his soldiers. Of the men buried at Vilnius, one of the army's stopping-off points, none appears to have been killed in battle.

Battlefields of the First World War

During the First World War (1914–1918), millions of soldiers fought and died in the trenches of Europe. For a few people, this is still part of living memory. But for future generations, archaeological evidence will be one way of piecing together

▲ Trenches dug during the First World War were home to troops, such as these American soldiers at Verdun, France, for months at a time. The battlefields are still full of objects which provide archaeologists with information about how the soldiers spent their time in preparation for battle.

a picture of life in the trenches. The sites of some of the major battles, such as Ypres, Verdun, the Somme and Passchendale, still contain the grim evidence of warfare.

Battlefield archaeology can help tell forgotten stories, too. Excavations in the late 1990s discovered evidence of a First World War trench system at Bosinghe in Belgium. The remains of more than 120 soldiers were also discovered, revealing for the first time the presence of a battlefield that had been overlooked and largely forgotten by history.

▼ The army of the Sioux, Cheyenne and Arapaho people, ferocious and nimble in battle, easily outmanoeuvred Custer's men. Armed not only with their traditional weapons but also with the latest and most sophisticated semi-automatic rifles, they succeeded in putting the 7th Cavalry to flight.

City of London

The City of London today is one of the great financial and trading centres of the world. In its long history, successive civilizations have thrived there. It has been built and rebuilt many times and is a city of many archaeological layers. Some evidence of London's past can be seen above ground, but by digging through its underground layers archaeologists have uncovered a wealth of evidence which tells us the fascinating story of the city and its people.

▲▶ The elegant dome of St. Paul's Cathedral (top left), built between 1675 and 1710 after the Great Fire of London, sits alongside today's modern office blocks and commercial buildings. Layered beneath the city are many more remains of London's long history.

▼ London is rich in artefacts from Roman times. Archaeologists have unearthed a first-century well made of barrels, pieces of high-quality glassware, jewellery, crockery and a writing tablet recording the sale of a slave-girl, Fortunata, in c. CE80–120. Objects from later centuries include a hoard of gold coins issued to hospital patients by King Henry VIII (ruled CE1509–1547).

Roman Londinium

The area now covered by London was once countryside, and there is evidence of farming settlements dating back 15,000 years. In the city itself, the deepest (and earliest) major layers are Roman, dating from the 1st century CE. The Romans were the first to build a bridge across the River Thames, and they built up the city to be a trading centre of the Roman Empire. Archaeologists have excavated many Roman sites and uncovered the remains of ruined bathhouses, temples and houses. They have unearthed hundreds of small artefacts, including, in 2003, a jar of face cream with the finger marks of its owner still visible!

Medieval London

The Romans left in CE410 after their rule collapsed. The area was abandoned for many centuries, but London became an Anglo-Saxon centre in the 9th century, and later fell to the Vikings, then the Normans. By the 14th century, the thriving medieval city had become the capital of England. Craftspeople, from goldsmiths and grocers to butchers and bell-makers, were powerful, and have left countless traces of their activities. Under Queen Elizabeth I (ruled 1558–1603), London prospered still further, becoming a bustling city of commerce and entertainment. Archaeologists have discovered the remains of the Rose Theatre, where some of William Shakespeare's plays were first performed.

The Great Fire

On 2 September 1666, disaster struck the city. A fire that had started in a baker's shop in a narrow medieval street spread quickly throughout the adjoining timber houses. Four days later it had destroyed over 13,000 houses and 87 churches. Excavations in this area regularly expose a thick deposit of charcoal and baked clay relating to the fire.

The modern city rises

After the Great Fire, London was rebuilt once more. A new St. Paul's Cathedral replaced the one destroyed in the blaze. The street plans laid out after the fire, with wide roads and spacious squares replacing the cramped medieval streets, became the basis of modern London. Today, in the heart of the city, gleaming skyscrapers tower above the public buildings erected in the years since the fire. And as the foundations of a new building are dug, earlier levels of the past come to light – a clay pipe from an 18th-century coffee house, a 17th-century helmet from a soldier of the English Civil War, a statue to the Roman god Mithras, or a flint axe-head from a time we can barely imagine.

▼ In 4th-century Londinium, wealthy merchants lived in splendid, well-decorated town houses. The Bucklersbury Pavement, a mosaic floor found near the Bank of England, is a good example. This small area at the heart of London has been the focus of activity for merchants and traders for centuries.

SUMMARY OF CHAPTER 2: TOUCHING THE PAST

The thrill of discovery

People die but things remain. The houses, cities and monuments people build can endure for thousands of years. Sometimes these buildings are remarkably well-preserved after centuries, sometimes they are very run-down or hidden under vegetation or beneath later structures. In this chapter we have uncovered the secrets of some of the most exciting and famous archaeological sites in the world. These places have fascinated generations of archaeologists. Some have been lucky enough to discover famous sites for themselves, and to experience the thrill of being the first person to set eyes on something that had been hidden for centuries. Others have

Aztec feathered shield (c. CE1466–1520) depicting a mythical water creature

looked closer at sites that have already been excavated. All have shared in the excitement of contributing more to our understanding of life in times gone by.

More and more clues

As we have seen in this chapter, archaeological sites hold all sorts of clues, big and small, which help archaeologists to build up a picture of the people who lived there and the lives they led. The jars found at Tutankhamun's tomb, the preserved food and graffiti at Pompeii, sailors' personal property on the *Mary Rose* and spent ammunition at the battlefield at Little Bighorn – all are just as important in terms of what they tell us as the big, spectacular buildings. Perhaps there is a site near you where artefacts have been unearthed which tell a story about the place in times past. If you go to a local museum or join a local archaeology society you are sure to find out all sorts of exciting information archaeologists have pieced together. And what about the objects you use and throw away? One day these objects may be studied by archaeologists of the future. What stories will they tell?

Go further...

Play games based on the ancient Egyptians, Greeks, Romans and Aztecs: http://www.gridclub.com/ have_a_go/history/history.shtml

Find a list of World Heritage Sites at: http://whc.unesco.org/heritage. htm#debut

Digging up the Past: Pompeii and Herculaneum by Peter Hicks (Hodder Children's Books, 1995)

Valley of the Kings (Digging for the Past) by Smith and Bernard (Oxford University Press, 2003)

Archaeology is Rubbish by Tony Robinson and Mick Aston (Channel 4 Books, 2003)

Architectural historian
Studies the styles and construction of ancient buildings.

Conservationist
Specialises in preserving ancient things from frescoes and furniture to palaces and temples.

Custodian
Controls galleries and archaeological sites to keep them safe from damage and theft, and looks after displays so that members of the public can visit.

Film maker or documentary maker
Uses history and archaeology as a starting point for their imaginations in re-creating past worlds on film or television.

Visit the Museum of London for a trip through time, exploring London from its prehistoric origins to the present day:
Museum of London,
London Wall,
London EC2Y 5HN, UK.
Telephone: +44 (0) 870 444 3851
www.museumoflondon.org.uk

See the Mary Rose:
Portsmouth Historic Dockyard,
Portsmouth, UK.
Telephone: +44 (0) 23 9281 2931
www.maryrose.org

Explore the Acropolis at the Acropolis Museum, Athens, Greece:
www.culture.gr/2/21/211/21101m/ e211am01.html

Glossary

aerial photography
A method of studying a site through photographs taken from the air.

afterlife
Eternal or everlasting life after death. Most religions and cultures believe in some form of afterlife.

alignment
A row of objects positioned so as to be in line with something else, such as the rising sun or the moon and stars at particular times of the year.

amphitheatre
A semicircular space used for public performances and surrounded by tiers of seats, invented by the ancient Greeks.

amulet
A type of ornament worn as a charm against evil spirits.

Anglo-Saxon
Belonging to a period of English history from the end of the Roman empire (CE476) to the Norman invasion (CE1066).

aqueduct
A bridge-like structure built to channel water from place to place.

archaeology
The study of the past using careful analysis and scientific examination of material remains, carried out by archaeologists.

artefact
An object made by humans.

artillery
Heavy weapons. Also the part of an army that uses artillery in battle.

Aztecs
People of the Aztec civilization, dominant in Mexico from the 12th to the 16th century CE.

BCE
Before Common Era: a non-religious dating system in which 1BCE is equivalent to 1BC.

Bronze Age
The second stage in a three-stage classification of prehistoric time, when people started to use bronze in the making of weapons and tools. In Europe this happened between c. 3000BCE and 800BCE.

burial mound
A mound of earth or stones containing the bodies of the dead.

carbon dating
A scientific method of dating an organic object such as wood, other plant remains or human remains.

cave art
Pictures painted or etched onto the walls of caves by prehistoric people.

CE
Common Era: a non-religious dating system in which CE1 is equivalent to AD1.

celestial
Relating to the sky or heavens.

citadel
A defensive fortification built high off the ground to protect a town or city from attack.

civilization
A highly advanced culture or society.

commerce
Buying and selling.

conquistador
One of the Spanish soldier-adventurers who conquered much of south and central America in the 16th century CE.

crusader
A participant in one of the military expeditions led by European Christians to seize Jerusalem from the Muslims between the 11th and 13th centuries CE.

currency
Something used as a medium of exchange when buying and selling – usually, though not always, money.

dig
An archaeological excavation.

DNA
A chemical found inside all living things. It carries information that is unique to each individual, but similar in individuals who are related to each other. Scientists can examine the DNA in ancient human remains and find out if bodies found near each other were related.

empire
A collection of countries ruled by another country and its leaders.

excavation
The process of digging up a site to find archaeological evidence.

fertility
When referring to land, plants or crops, the ability to produce abundant harvests.

flint
A hard stone used for making early prehistoric tools and weapons.

fortifications
Defensive structures, such as walls and moats, built to protect a settlement from attack.

fortress
A heavily fortified structure.

foundations
The supporting level of stone, brick or concrete on which structures are built. Often the remains of foundations last after buildings have fallen down or been destroyed.

fragment
A small part detached from a larger object.

fresco
A wall painting.

frieze
A decorative strip painted or sculpted along the top edge of a wall.

funerary
Relating to a funeral.

geophysics
The study of the earth's physical properties. Geophysics can help archaeologists work out where there are structures lying underground.

hallucinogenic
Causing unusual dreams or visions.

hieroglyphs
Picture-writing invented by the ancient Egyptians.

hull
The main body of a ship.

hunter-gatherer
A member of a small nomadic community living by hunting, fishing and collecting wild food such as honey, nuts and berries.

Incas
The people of the central Andes region of South America whose empire was at its height in the 15th century CE.

Iron Age
The third prehistoric period of classification, when iron was used to make tools and weapons. In Europe this was from c. 800BCE until the beginning of the Roman period (c. 100BCE).

keel
The timber or metal base of a ship – the part that is below the water line.

legend
A traditional story which does not necessarily have a firm basis in historical fact.

Mayan
Relating to the civilization and people of southern Mexico between c. CE300 and CE900.

medieval
Relating to the Middle Ages of European history, from about the 5th to the 15th century CE.

megalith
A large prehistoric stone monument found in northern Europe.

metropolis
A very large city.

Moors
The Arab Muslims of north Africa who colonized Spain between the 8th and 15th centuries CE.

mosque
A place of worship for Muslim people.

mummy
A preserved human body. It may have been preserved deliberately, such as in the case of ancient Egyptian mummies, or under certain conditions it may have been preserved naturally.

myth
A legend or traditional story, often involving gods and goddesses or other supernatural beings, and usually culturally very important to the society to which it belongs.

native American
Relating to the earliest inhabitants of North and South America and their descendants, rather than settlers who arrived from Europe from the 15th century CE onwards.

nomad
A member of a community moving from place to place without settling permanently.

Norman conquest
The conquest of England by the Normans, led by King William I, in CE1066.

palaeolithic
Relating to the early Stone Age, a vast period of time stretching from about 2.5 million years ago, when the first artefacts were made, to around 13,000BCE.

passage grave
A tomb reached by moving along a horizontal passage. Passage graves were commonly built in northern Europe in around 3000BCE.

pharaoh
An ancient Egyptian ruler.

plaza
A square or formal space in a town or city.

prehistory
The time before written records existed. This period varies around the world because writing was developed at different times by different cultures.

pueblo
Relating to the native American peoples of New Mexico and Arizona, USA, and their culture.

pyramid
A monument which is square at the base and pointed at the top. The most famous pyramids are the ancient Egyptian tombs.

radar
A method of finding objects by sending out radio waves and analyzing their echoes.

radioactivity
Energy generated by the disintegration of atoms (tiny particles from which all substances are made) over time.

ramparts
High defensive boundaries running around the edge of a fortified building, town or city.

replica
A copy of something.

ritual
A formal (often religious) action performed in a solemn way.

rosary
A string of beads used to aid devotion during prayer.

sacrifice
The killing of an animal or person as an offering to a higher power or god.

satellite imaging
The use of satellite technology to provide overhead views of archaeological sites. Satellite images often show patterns of structures under the ground.

settlement
A place where a group of people live together for a lengthy period of time. Farms, villages, towns, cities and palaces are all settlements.

shrine
A special place set aside to honour a person or a god.

Stone Age
The first (and earliest) of the three classifications of prehistory, when stone was used for tools and weapons. It is a long period of time dating back to the earliest origins of humankind. In Europe it ended after 3000BCE, when the Bronze Age began.

strata (singular: stratum)
Layers of material left behind by people or things at successive times in history and prehistory. The study of these various levels of material helps archaeologists date the objects they find.

Sumerian
Relating to the ancient Mesopotamian civilization of Sumer, which began to develop around 3000BCE, and its people. Ur was one of the Sumerian city-states.

temple
A building constructed for religious worship.

terracotta
Baked clay often used to make ornaments, pottery and statues.

trench
A long, narrow ditch. Archaeologists often dig trenches as part of their excavation of a site. Trenches were also a feature of battlefields in the First World War, where they served as a place of shelter for soldiers and a location for the fighting itself.

urban
Relating to a town or city.

Viking
One of the Scandinavian warriors who invaded Europe between the 8th and 11th centuries CE.

X-ray
A type of radiation used to reveal things hidden beneath something else, such as bones in a person's body or a mummy inside a stone coffin.

ziggurat
A step-sided pyramid prominent in the cityscapes of ancient Mesopotamia.

Index

Acknowledgements

The publisher would like to thank the following for permission to reproduce their material.
Every care has been taken to trace copyright holders. However, if there have been unintentional
omissions or failure to trace copyright holders, we apologize and will, if informed, endeavour
to make corrections in any future edition.

Key: *b* = bottom, *c* = centre, *l* = left, *r* = right, *t* = top

Cover *l* Art Archive; Cover *c* Art Archive; Cover *r* Art Archive; Cover *background* Getty; 1 Corbis;
2 3 Corbis 4 5 Corbis; 7 Getty; 8*tl* Pitt Rivers Museum, Oxford; 8*cr* Corbis; 9*t* AKG, London;
10–11 Corbis; 12*tl* Science Photo Library (SPL); 12*bl* Art Archive; 12–13 Skyscan; 13*br* Art Archive;
14*cr* Art Archive; 14*bl* Corbis; 14–15 Art Archive; 15*t* Corbis; 15*b* Art Archive; 16*tl* Art Archive;
17*t* British Museum; 18*tl* Corbis; 18*bl* National Geographic Image Collection; 19*tc* Getty News;
19*bc* Rex Features; 19*r* Corbis; 20–21*t* Corbis; 20*bl* SPL; 21*tc* Corbis; 21*bl* David Ford; 22*cl* British
Museum; 23*t* British Museum; 24*tl* Art Archive; 24*bl* Corbis; 25*tr* Corbis; 25*b* Corbis; 26*tl* Art Archive;
26*cr* Art Archive; 28*tl* Art Archive; 28*bl* Corbis; 28–29 Art Archive; 29*t* Michael Fox; 29*b* Alamy;
30–31 Corbis; 31*c* Hulton Getty; 31*tcl* Art Archive; 32*tl* British Museum; 32*bl* British Museum;
34*tl* Bridgeman Art Library; 34*cr* British Museum; 34*bl* Corbis; 35 Corbis; 36–37 Art Archive; 36*br* Corbis;
37*tr* Corbis; 37*br* Getty; 38*tl* Alamy; 38–39 Art Archive; 39*b* Art Archive; 40*tl* Art Archive; 40*cr* NGIC;
40*b* Corbis; 41*tr* Corbis; 41*b* Corbis; 42*tl* AKG, London; 42*b* AKG, London; 43*l* Corbis; 43*tr* Corbis;
43*br* Corbis; 44*l* Corbis; 44–45 Corbis; 45*tr* Corbis; 46*tr* Werner Foreman Archive; 47*tr* Corbis;
48*tr* Werner Foreman Archive; 48*b* Art Archive; 49*l* Art Archive; 49*tr* Corbis; 50*tl* Scala; 50*cr* Art Archive;
51*tr* David Hiser/Aspen Photographers; 52*tl* The Mary Rose Trust; 52*bl* The Mary Rose Trust; 52–53 Art
Archive; 53*tr* Corbis; 54*tl* Art Archive; 54*bl* Corbis; 54–55 Corbis; 55*tr* Corbis; 55*cl* Corbis; 55*br* Corbis;
58*cl* Art Archive; 59*br* Corbis; 60*b* Corbis; 62–63 Corbis; 64 Corbis

The publisher would like to thank the following illustrators:
Roger Hutchins 31; Steve Weston (Linden Artists) 8–9, 11, 16–17, 26–27,
32–33, 36, 46–47, 50–51, 56–57.

The author would like to thank Catherine for the care and hard work she put into editing the text
and Pete for the design. Not forgetting Gill who commissioned the book in the first place.

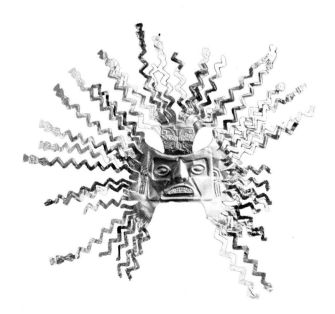